A Toe
in the Water

A Comedy

Derek Benfield

Samuel French - London
New York - Toronto - Hollywood

A TOE IN THE WATER

First presented at the Contra-Kreis Theater in Bonn on November 30th, 1989, with the following cast of characters:

Gerald	Thomas Wenske
Rodney	Til Schweiger
Linda	Carolin van Bergen
Sandra	Adelheid Kleineidam
Potter	Gerd Neubert
Marion	Karyn von Ostholt

The play directed by Horst Johanning
Setting by Pit Fischer

The action takes place in various parts of a health farm during Summer

ACT I   A Friday afternoon
ACT II   A few minutes later

Time—the present

Other plays by Derek Benfield published by Samuel French Ltd

ACT I

A health farm in a delightful part of the country

The audience are, so to speak, sitting in the swimming-pool and in the downstage area there is a sun lounger C and a colourful padded seat DR. A swing door DR leads into the steam baths and sauna, with a white wicker basket for used towels nearby

An archway DL leads to the bedrooms and to the pool (if an entrance from the audience is not possible). There is another archway UR through which you go out to your L to the main entrance, and to your R to the massage parlour and the doctor's office. Beyond the poolside area is a bedroom which has a door UL leading to the corridor, another UC to the bathroom, and a practical sash window. (The bedroom is on the first floor.) On the L of the window is a small recessed wardrobe cupboard. In the bedroom is a divan bed with a bedside table above it on which is a lamp and the telephone, and a small armchair to the R with a table below it. If possible the bedroom should be raised slightly above the poolside area. (In Act 2 the bedroom will serve as two different bedrooms on different occasions, the number on the outside of the door being changed as required)

The Lights come up in the pool area. A faint green glow shimmers from the swimming-pool. Gentle, soothing music is being piped through. It is altogether a peaceful, relaxing scene

There is quite a pause

Then the door to the steam bath bursts open abruptly and Gerald staggers out amidst a puff of steam. He is a forthright, middle-aged man, nouveau riche, a builder by trade and a little bit of a snob. He is wrapped in a large towel, red in the face and gasping for breath. He throws a spare towel into the basket and steadies himself, relieved to be out of the inferno. He groans a little, exhausted by the heat. He drifts, exhausted, across to the sun lounger, sinks on to it and disappears into his vast towel as he tries to recover. The music continues, peacefully ...

Rodney wanders in from the archway UR looking about, apprehensively. He is young, very good-looking, normally a perky working-class boy with an eye for the girls, but at the moment lacking in confidence in the strange surroundings in which he finds himself. He is wearing casual clothes and carries a small weekend bag. He is wearing sun-glasses

Rodney looks about, lifts his sun-glasses a little to get a better look. He is surprised and bewildered by his surroundings and looks about in awe

He does not notice the figure wrapped in towelling, and wanders down to peer into the swimming-pool (the audience). Then he notices the door to the steam baths. He goes towards it, puzzled, wondering to where it leads. He reaches one hand out, tentatively, and is about to open the door when——

From within the towelling on the seat a voice startles him

Gerald Aren't you going to take your trousers off?

Rodney jumps, nervously, and turns to look in the direction of the voice

Rodney Sorry?

Gerald's head thrusts out from the towel like a tortoise from its shell

Gerald Not *many* people go into the steam bath fully-clothed.
Rodney (*appalled*) Steam bath?!
Gerald Through there.
Rodney Is that what it is?
Gerald Steam bath and sauna.
Rodney Good lord ... !
Gerald Isn't that what you came for? The treatment?
Rodney (*horrified*) No!
Gerald (*abruptly*) Ah!!
Rodney (*jumping again*) What?

Gerald glares at him, suspiciously

Gerald You're here for something *else*!
Rodney Yes ... (*He smiles, sheepishly*)
Gerald (*abruptly*) About time, too! Where the hell have you been?

Rodney consults his watch

Rodney I'm only two hours late.
Gerald (*snorting*) Two *days* more like! People could be dropping dead in there.
Rodney What?!
Gerald So you can forget what I said about taking your clothes off.
Rodney Can I?
Gerald Doesn't apply to you. Plumbers are exempt.
Rodney Plumbers?

Gerald rises like Lazarus in his mound of towelling

Gerald Well, don't hang about here gossiping now you *have* arrived! Roll up your sleeves and get to work.
Rodney Look, I think you've made a——
Gerald (*crossing to the steam bath*) That steam bath has developed a mind of its own. The pipes are practically bursting. If it gets any hotter we'll end up in orbit.
Rodney I'm not a plumber!

Gerald turns and glares at him, balefully

Gerald Well, if you're not a plumber and you're not here for the treatment what the hell *are* you here for?
Rodney I'm ... I'm meeting somebody.
Gerald An assignation?! In *this* place?
Rodney Yes. *I* thought it was a bit odd, too ...
Gerald Then why did you book it?
Rodney I didn't! *She* did!
Gerald Who?
Rodney My girl-friend.
Gerald You're meeting a *girl*? *Here*?!
Rodney Yes ...

Gerald laughs, noisily

Gerald Oh, well, perhaps you'd *better* take your clothes off, then. (*He opens the door to the steam bath and groans*) Ugh ... !
Rodney You're not going back in there?
Gerald Certainly. I've *paid* for it, haven't I?

Gerald goes out into the steam bath amidst a puff of steam and closes the door behind him

A voice from behind startles Rodney again

Linda (*off*) Rodney!!
Rodney Aaaah!

He jumps a mile, hastily replaces his dark glasses and holds up his weekend bag in front of his chest like a shield

Linda has come in from UR. She is a very pretty, educated, well-spoken girl of about twenty-four with a warm attractive personality. The only thing she is wearing is a bath towel wrapped around her shapely form like a sarong

Linda Where have you *been*?

Rodney peers at her, short-sightedly, through his steamed up dark glasses

(*Patiently*) I should take them off if I were you.
Rodney Sorry?
Linda Your sun-glasses! Then you might recognize me.

Rodney lowers his head and peers over the top of his glasses

It's *me*—Linda!
Rodney I know who it is! I just didn't think you'd be dressed like that.
Linda Everybody here dresses like this.
Rodney (*surprised*) Do they?
Linda It's quite usual.
Rodney Blimey ... !
Linda (*impulsively*) Anyway—you're here—that's the main thing! Oh, darling!

She runs to him to embrace him, but his weekend bag is in her way. She backs off and tries again. He shifts the bag a little, but again she collides with it.

Finally, he lifts it above his head to let her in. They embrace, she enthusiastically, he nervously, the bag now resting against her bottom. They remain in each other's arms

Linda I expected you hours ago.
Rodney I couldn't find the bloody place!
Linda You are hopeless. I knew I should have drawn you a map.
Rodney I was looking for an hotel! You never said you were going to book us into a health farm.

Linda tries to withdraw from their embrace, but is still trapped by the weekend bag. He lifts it above his head again to release her

Linda I thought it was a good idea.
Rodney Why?
Linda Well, you know what my father is!
Rodney (*puzzled*) What's your father got to do with you and me coming to stay on a health farm?
Linda (*embarrassed*) Well ... he's very fussy about who I go out with ...
Rodney You mean he wouldn't approve of you going out with *me*?
Linda Oh, Rodney, you mustn't think badly of him!
Rodney Sorry?
Linda He only wants what's best for me.
Rodney So he wouldn't want you going away with a window-cleaner?
Linda (*appalled at the idea*) No, of course he wouldn't!
Rodney And that's why you booked us into this place?
Linda Well, I thought it would be more discreet. Daddy doesn't know about health farms, so he'd never find us here.
Rodney Thank God for that ... !
Linda Rodney——
Rodney What?
Linda *I'm* not like my father.
Rodney Oh, good!
Linda I *like* window-cleaners ...
Rodney I hoped you would.
Linda Come on! (*She takes his hand*)
Rodney Where are we going?
Linda *You're* going to take your clothes off.
Rodney I thought you'd never ask!

Linda laughs and leads him out towards the bedrooms

As they go the door to the steam bath bursts open again and Gerald staggers out as before, wrapped in a towel, red in the face and gasping for breath

He throws a spare towel into the wicker basket and drifts, unsteadily, across to sink on to the sun lounger again, disappearing from sight amongst the towelling

A swell of lush, romantic music (preferably "Love is a Many-Splendoured Thing") heralds the arrival of Sandra out of the swimming-pool (i.e. the audience, if possible). She is a jolly girl in her twenties, very pretty but rather plump. Not that this bothers Sandra, who sees herself as slim and sexy. She is breathing heavily after her swim, and is looking towards the recumbent figure on the sun lounger and smiling, mischievously. She picks up a towel from the seat and starts to dry herself as she tiptoes across towards the mound of towelling. She bends down close to Gerald and says—

Sandra Mr Corby ...

The mound of towelling jumps a mile

Gerald Aaaah!!

The music stops. Gerald parts his towel and peers out, cautiously. He comes face-to-face with Sandra, and reacts in alarm

Oh, my God ...! (*He closes the towel over his face again, quickly*)

Sandra (*in assumed surprise*) Mr Corby—it's *you*!

Gerald (*from within the towelling*) No, it isn't!

Sandra Well, it's somebody just *like* you.

Gerald (*looking out again*) Yes—my twin brother! *I'm* not here at all! (*He gets up, quickly, and starts to escape, but trips over the end of his towel and falls to the ground*) Oh, blast ...!

Sandra (*in apparent surprise*) Well! Fancy you and me coming to the same health farm ...

Gerald (*grimly*) Yes—what a coincidence! (*He scrambles to his feet, clutching his towel around him to preserve his dignity*)

Sandra (*going to him, smiling happily*) Whatever will they think at the office when they know that we were both here at the same time?

Gerald Well, *I* won't tell them if *you* don't! Anyhow, it isn't as if we came here *together*, is it?

Sandra No, but——

Gerald (*pointedly*) Or as if we were going to spend any time together.

Sandra We *might* ...

Gerald We mustn't!

Sandra Why not? We spend a lot of time together in the office.

Gerald That's different! You're sitting at a typewriter with your clothes on and I'm not dressed in a towel!

Sandra (*giggling*) Wouldn't it be funny if we dressed like this in the office?

Gerald Yes. *Very* funny. We could charge admission. (*The snob in him emerges*) Wait a minute—how can you afford this place on the money *I* pay you?

Sandra I've been saving.

Gerald Well, it's no good, Sandra. You'll have to go.

Sandra Why?

Gerald Because I'm supposed to be relaxing, that's why!

Sandra (*seductively*) I can help you relax ...

Gerald Oh, no, you can't!

Sandra It'll be nice for you to have female company, Mr Corby ...

Gerald No, it won't! I came here for peace and quiet.

Sandra Well, we don't have to be noisy ...

Gerald (*brooding*) It'll never be the same in the office now. How will I be able to look you in the face across the fax machine after this?

Sandra (*hopefully*) Why? What are we going to do?
Gerald Nothing! We're not going to do nothing—*any*thing!
Sandra Oh, what a pity. (*She starts to go*)
Gerald Where are you going?
Sandra (*touched*) Aah ... you're going to miss me.
Gerald 'Course I'm not!
Sandra I'm going to get a hot drink after my swim.
Gerald Oh ...
Sandra Do *you* want one?
Gerald No fear!

Sandra continues on her way. He has a sudden thought

Here—wait a minute!
Sandra Yes?
Gerald You *knew* I was coming here. You typed the letter confirming my
    booking.
Sandra Yes ...
Gerald So why did *you* go and book at the same place?

Sandra smiles at him, sheepishly

Sandra You would have been awfully lonely all on your own, Mr Corby ...

 She goes out through the archway UR

Gerald Oh, my God ... !

*He sinks, disconsolately, back on to the sun lounger and disappears into his
towel*

The Lights come up in the bedroom ...

 *Rodney and Linda come in. We see there is a number "10" on the door.
 Linda closes the door*

Linda Well? What do you think?
Rodney (*gazing at her, entranced*) Beautiful ... !
Linda (*laughing*) The room!
Rodney Oh. (*He looks about*) It's a bit dark.
Linda You've still got your sun-glasses on!
Rodney Oh. (*He removes them and pretends to be blinded by the light*)
    Ooooooh! (*He throws himself on to the bed, dramatically*)
Linda You're crazy. ...

 She laughs and goes into the bathroom

*Rodney grins. He gets up and hastily and untidily unpacks some of the things
from his bag, distributing them haphazardly about the place, humming happily*

Rodney (*calling*) You know, this is the first time I've ever done this.
Linda (*off*) Done what?
Rodney Shared a room with a girl on a health farm! (*He sees something out
    of the window that alarms him*) Oh, my God ... ! (*Calling*) Linda!
Linda (*off*) Just coming!

Linda comes back in. She is now wearing a bikini and carrying a beach towel

What's the matter?

Rodney Look at them out there! (*As Linda approaches he notices her bikini*) Oh—are we going swimming?

Linda Why not? (*She looks out of the window, calmly*)

Rodney What the hell are they doing?

Linda Exercises, of course.

Rodney (*alarmed*) Exercises? Why?

Linda It's good for you! *I* should be out there with them, but I said I was waiting for you.

Rodney (*appalled*) You mean *we* have to do that?

Linda Every afternoon.

Rodney (*moving away*) I don't think I'm going to like it here. . . . If you'd left it to me I'd have booked us into the *Holiday Inn*.

Linda (*following him*) If I'd left it to you we'd never have gone anywhere! You *will* like it Rodney . . .

Rodney (*sulking a little*) No, I won't . . .

Linda You *will* . . .

Rodney Will I?

Linda (*romantically*) Well . . . we are together, aren't we? Just the two of us.

Rodney What about that lot out there?

Linda In *here* there's just the two of us.

Rodney Is there? (*He counts them*) One, two. Yes, you're right.

He closes to her and they kiss. He tries to move towards the bed, but she restrains him

Linda Where are we going?

Rodney I don't like it standing up.

Linda Rodney . . . !

Rodney I'm tired. I've had a long journey. I need rest.

Linda (*doubtfully*) Oh, yes . . . ?

He grins, guiltily, and tries again to lead her towards the bed. Again she restrains him

No.

Rodney What?

Linda You can't do that now.

Rodney I thought that was the idea.

Linda There's plenty of time.

Rodney No, there isn't. Tomorrow we'll be out there doing exercises! So come on! (*He tries again*)

Linda No, Rodney!

Rodney No?

Linda You're not allowed to.

Rodney Sorry?

Linda You've only just arrived.

Rodney What's that got to do with it?

Linda Well ... you've got to be weighed first.

Rodney thinks about this for a moment and smiles in total disbelief

Rodney I beg your pardon?
Linda They weigh you first.
Rodney Do they?
Linda Yes. Before and after.
Rodney Before and after?!
Linda Yes.

He laughs, uncertainly

Rodney Don't be daft!
Linda They have to know how much you weigh before you start and when you finish.
Rodney They'd never have done that at the *Holiday Inn* ... !
Linda *And* they have to keep an eye on your blood pressure.
Rodney (*modestly*) Well, there's bound to be a bit of heavy breathing ...
Linda Then they enter it all on your card.
Rodney What card?
Linda Your record card.
Rodney You mean they're going to keep a record?!
Linda (*patiently*) Rodney, that's what we're paying them for.
Rodney To keep a record of everything we do?
Linda It won't make any difference to *us*.
Rodney Won't it?
Linda Of course not.
Rodney Oh. Well, that's all right, then.
Linda So now you go in there and take your clothes off.

Rodney grins

Rodney I'd forgotten all about that! I'll do it now. (*He starts to go towards the bathroom*)
Linda I'll be downstairs by the swimming-pool.

He stops and turns

Rodney But I'm just taking my clothes off.
Linda Yes.
Rodney Well ... don't you want to stay?
Linda Why? Do you need an audience?
Rodney (*sheepishly*) I ... I just thought you'd be staying.
Linda What's the matter? Can't you manage on your own?
Rodney Of course I can manage!
Linda That's all right, then. So as soon as you've got undressed, go down to the office and get yourself weighed. (*She opens the door to the corridor*) See you by the pool!

She blows him a kiss and goes

Rodney Oh, hell ... !

He picks up his weekend case and goes, miserably, out into the bathroom

In the pool area ...

Gerald is still deep in his towel

Mr Potter enters urgently from the archway UR, *looking for someone. He is a primly respectable, highly moral man, suffering under the burden of responsibility and almost totally devoid of humour. He is wearing trainers, track suit trousers and a tee-shirt bearing the health farm logo. He is carrying a clipboard on which are various documents. He looks about, anxiously*

Potter Mr Corby! Mr Corby! (*He sees the recumbent Gerald*) Ah! (*He goes to him*) Mr Corby—she's ready for you ...

Gerald lies doggo, hoping that Potter will go away. But Potter remains

It's no good pretending. I know you're in there somewhere. (*He tries to pull the towelling apart, searching for Gerald*)
Gerald (*muffled*) Go away ... !
Potter (*plaintively*) But what about Mrs Maddock? You don't want to keep Mrs Maddock waiting, do you?
Gerald (*muffled*) Yes, I do ... !
Potter But she's so *good* for you, sir! You know you always feel better after you've been with Mrs Maddock.

Gerald's head appears

Gerald What are you talking about?
Potter Massage! It's part of the treatment. It's what you're paying us for. (*Piously*) We can't take your money if you don't have the treatment, now can we?
Gerald Well, knock ten per cent off my bill and cancel the massage! (*He disappears back into the towelling*)
Potter Oh, Mr Corby, you will have your little joke ... !

Gerald's head re-appears

Gerald Look, Potter—being here is supposed to be a pleasure.

Potter hastily quietens him, appalled at the word

Potter S'sh! S'sh! (*He looks about, fearful that Gerald has been overheard*) I hope you didn't come here for. ... *pleasure*?
Gerald Why not? It's costing me enough!

Potter closes his eyes, sorrowfully ...

Potter Oh, no, sir—this is a health farm, not a holiday camp. Enjoyment here comes from physical fitness. (*He runs on the spot for a moment*)

Gerald watches him, balefully

Gerald Are you telling me that I'm supposed to *suffer*?

Potter A small price to pay for physical health. (*He leans closer to Gerald*) And physical health, as you and I know, sir, is the first step to *moral* health.

Gerald There's nothing wrong with *my* morals!

Potter Ah—no! Of course not! I didn't mean to suggest——

Gerald Anyhow, I don't think I've got the strength to face Mrs Maddock's massage. Not after that steam bath! It's like a blasted inferno in there. You'll have people passing out soon. I thought you were getting a plumber?

Potter (*unhappily*) I have *tried*, sir ...

Gerald And failed!

Potter I've telephoned them three times. But plumbers' promises are paper thin. I was *hoping* ... (*He peters out*)

Gerald Hoping?

Potter Well ... *you*, sir.

Gerald *Me*, sir?

Potter Yes, sir. You are a ... builder, after all.

Gerald glowers at him

Gerald I thought I was here for my physical and moral health, not to mess about with pipes!

Potter Ah—no! Of course not! I shouldn't have asked. I do apologize.

Gerald (*loftily*) I'm an employer, not an employee.

Potter Quite so, sir. (*Hopefully*) Well ... ? Shall we ... er ... ? (*He moves his arms from side to side, almost as if about to dance*) Shall we ... er ... ?

Gerald Dance?

Potter No, no!

Gerald What, then?

Potter Mrs Maddock's waiting!

Gerald Well, she can go *on* waiting. I'd rather stay here. (*He settles down into his towel*)

Potter flutters about him like an agitated butterfly

Potter But it's all a balanced programme! It has to go like clockwork!

Gerald Potter ...

Potter People have got to do what I ask them to do! At the time that I ask them to do it!

Gerald Potter!

Potter And if they don't—(*getting near to tears*)—then my whole edifice will start to crumble!

Gerald (*loudly*) Potter!!

Potter controls himself

You don't have to go raving mad ... (*He rises, reluctantly*) All right. If I must, I must.

Potter (*cheering up immediately*) Oh, *thank* you, sir! Follow me!

Gerald (*as they go*) I'd rather be massaged by Mrs Maddock than stay here and watch your edifice crumbling ...

They disappear through the archway UR. *As they go, Linda is coming in from the bedrooms, carrying her towel. She looks into the swimming-pool (the audience), and is about to put a toe in the water as——*

Sandra returns with a mug of Bovril. She is expecting to find Gerald where she left him

Sandra There! That didn't take very long, did it? (*She stops, seeing Linda instead of Gerald*) Oh. Hallo.
Linda Hallo.

Sandra glances around, this way and that, wondering where Gerald can have gone to. Linda watches her in surprise

Have you lost somebody?
Sandra He was here a moment ago . . .
Linda Then I expect he'll be back in a minute.
Sandra I hope so . . . Have you just arrived?
Linda Yes.
Sandra Been before?
Linda No. My first time.
Sandra Me, too.
Linda Seems very nice.
Sandra Yes. On your own, are you?
Linda No. I'm here with a friend.
Sandra So am I. (*Pause*) In a way. (*Pause*) If he hasn't disappeared, that is . . .
Linda (*puzzled*) Sorry?
Sandra It was a bit of a secret. He didn't know I was going to be here.
Linda Oh. Must have been a nice surprise for him.
Sandra Well, I *hope* so . . .
Linda Have you known him very long?
Sandra He's my boss.
Linda (*amused*) Oh, I see . . .
Sandra So he's quite a bit older than I am. But he's very nice. Is . . . is yours an older man?
Linda Oh, no. Mine's quite young.
Sandra Oh. And pretty?
Linda H'm—*fairly* pretty.
Sandra You didn't find him *here*, did you?
Linda No. I brought mine with me.

They laugh

Potter walks in, briskly, from UR, *carrying his clipboard, crosses between them and goes out* DL

Sandra and Linda watch Potter in surprise

Sandra Well, I think I'll go and look for mine. I wonder where he's hiding himself . . . See you later!
Linda Right. I'm just going to have a swim.

Sandra is about to go, but hesitates . . .

Sandra Tell you what—if you get fed up with your young pretty one, perhaps we can swap half-way through?

Sandra giggles and goes out the way she came

Linda smiles and wanders off for her swim

In the bedroom . . .

Rodney is singing, happily, in the bathroom. A knock at the door. He does not hear it. The door opens and Potter peers in

Potter Are you there?

No response, so he comes into the room, tentatively

Is anybody there?

Rodney (*off*) Just coming, darling!

Rodney walks out of the bathroom. He is now wearing only a short, fluffy, very feminine dressing-gown (Linda's). He pirouettes to show it off, not seeing Potter

There you are! What do you think of that?

Potter looks aghast

Rodney completes his turn and sees Potter. He grabs the neck of the dressing-gown and holds it to his throat, modestly

Who the hell are you?

Potter (*smiling, proudly*) Mr Potter.

Rodney (*puzzled*) Who?

Potter The manager! (*Remonstrating gently*) You never came to see me . . .

Rodney Sorry?

Potter You were supposed to come and see me.

Rodney What for?

Potter To have a little talk about the things you'll be getting up to here.

Rodney (*laughing*) What's that got to do with you?

Potter Well, I like to explain exactly what it is that you'll be trying to achieve while you're staying here.

Rodney I *know* what I'll be trying to achieve!

Potter And after *we*'ve had our little talk I shall pass you on to the doctor.

Rodney Doctor?!

Potter We've got to be sure that you're fit for all the various activities.

Rodney (*blankly*) Pardon?

Potter Well, we can't have you over-exerting yourself if you're not up to it.

Rodney I *am* up to it! I don't want no doctor.

Potter But we must give you a check-up before you start.

Rodney What?!

Potter And if you're not completely fit there may be *some* things we won't allow you to do . . .

Rodney It's none of your business *what* I do!

Potter smiles wanly

Potter But we're responsible for you while you're here. We can't have you dropping dead half-way through, now can we, sir?
Rodney No—that would never do! (*He chuckles*) All right, then. Lead on!
Potter Ah! No!
Rodney Well, make up your mind!
Potter You can't go downstairs dressed like that! Why didn't you bring something more suitable?

Rodney looks down at his apparel, and chuckles

Rodney I didn't bring it! It's *hers*!
Potter (*mollified*) Ah—your *wife's*?
Rodney (*puzzled*) Wife? (*Remembering*) Ah—yes—*wife*! Right!
Potter Didn't you bring a dressing-gown of your own?
Rodney I didn't think I was going to need one! Does everyone here *really* wander about without their clothes on? Don't they even get dressed for dinner?
Potter (*with a bleak smile*) Oh, dinner here is hardly worth dressing up for. Not exactly Cordon Bleu. Thin soup. A little fruit ...
Rodney Oh, I see. More Garden of Eden.
Potter (*puzzled*) Garden of Eden?
Rodney Yes. An apple and a lot of heavy breathing! (*He laughs, raucously*)
Potter (*blankly*) Sorry? I don't think I quite ...
Rodney Oh, never mind ... !
Potter Perhaps you could put on something a little more ... substantial? (*He manages a faint smile*) This is not the *Folies Bergères*. (*He opens the door*)
Rodney All right, Mr Potter. I'll be there in five minutes. (*He starts to go*)
Potter Thank you, sir. (*He turns in the doorway*) You'll find *me* behind a green door marked "Private". It's next to a blue door marked "Doctor". That's where you'll find the doctor.

He goes, closing the door behind him

Rodney I'd never have guessed ... ! (*He opens the bathroom door*)

Potter's head re-appears

Potter What did you say?
Rodney Never mind!
Potter Right!

They both disappear, slamming their respective doors behind them in complete unison

In the pool area ...

Gerald is returning from his massage with a glass of orange juice. He is exhausted. He sips his orange juice, gratefully, puts the glass down on the

*garden table and staggers to the sun lounger. He sinks on to it with a moan
and disappears once again into his towelling*

*The same swell of lush, romantic music that heralded Sandra's arrival is
heard again as Linda returns from her swim. She is drying herself on her
towel and looking, apprehensively, towards the recumbent figure on the sun
lounger. She tiptoes across towards the mound of towelling, bends down
close to Gerald and says*

Linda Excuse me . . .

The mound of towelling jumps a mile

Gerald Aaaah!!

*The music stops. Gerald parts his towel and peers out, cautiously. He comes
face-to-face with Linda. They both react in alarm*

Oh, my God . . .! (*He closes the towel over his face again, quickly, gets up
and starts to escape, but trips over the end of his towel and falls to the
ground*) Oh, blast . . .!
Linda I—I don't believe it . . .! It *is* you . . .!
Gerald I wish it wasn't . . .!
Linda (*appalled*) Daddy!!
Gerald (*trying to sound pleased*) Linda!
Linda I saw you from the swimming pool. I couldn't believe it was you. But
it *is*, isn't it?
Gerald I think so . . .
Linda (*with forced enthusiasm*) What a lovely surprise!
Gerald Yes, isn't it?
Linda What are you doing here?

Gerald is still lying on the ground, uncomfortably

Gerald Trying to relax.
Linda You never *said* you were coming to a health farm.
Gerald Neither did you!

Potter comes in from DL, sees Gerald and goes to him, urgently

Potter Mr Corby! What are you doing down there? (*He pulls Gerald to his
feet*) You were supposed to be resting after Mrs Maddock's massage. (*He
tidies Gerald up, perfunctorily*)
Gerald (*gloomily*) I was! But I ran into someone I know . . . (*He looks at
Linda*)
Potter Really? (*Crossing to Linda*) What a lovely surprise!
Linda Yes. That's what *I* said . . .
Potter Have you known him very long?
Linda (*wearily*) Yes. Years and years and years . . .
Potter (*delightedly*) Well! Fancy coming here and meeting an old friend!
Linda He's not a friend. He's my father.

Potter clasps his hands together, ecstatically

Potter Your *father*? Oh, I do enjoy a happy family reunion.

Potter notices Linda's set face

You don't seem very pleased to see him ...

Linda It—it was so unexpected ...

Potter Well, aren't you going to say *hallo* to your dear father? (*He smiles, encouragingly*)

Linda Oh. Yes. Right. (*She goes to Gerald, gloomily*) Hallo, dear father. (*She kisses the top of his head, briefly*) Did *Mummy* know you were coming here?

Gerald 'Course she did!

Linda (*quietly*) Well, I wish she'd told *me* ... !

Gerald I didn't expect to find *you* in a place like this. It was quite a surprise, I can tell you.

Linda Didn't she want to come with you?

Gerald (*nervously*) Who?

Linda Mummy.

Gerald Oh. Oh, no! No, she doesn't fancy steam baths and starving.

Linda So you came here on your own?

Gerald stares at her, blankly, for a moment

Gerald Yes! Yes, of course I did! (*He changes the subject quickly*) You're here with a girl-friend, I suppose?

Linda Well ... not exactly.

Gerald So *you* came on your own as well?

Potter (*smiling, happily*) Oh, no, sir! *She's* not on her own.

Linda Yes, I am!

Potter (*surprised*) Sorry?

Linda (*going to him, urgently*) You know very well I am!

Potter No, I don't. You're here with your——

Linda No, I'm not!

Potter What?

Linda I haven't got one!

Potter But I met a young man——

Linda No, you didn't!

Potter Yes! Upstairs! He was wearing a——(*He mimes a short skirt*)

Linda No, he wasn't! You must have gone into the wrong room. You're mixing me up with someone else!

Potter Am I?

Linda Yes! *I'm* not here with *anyone*!

Potter looks bemused

Gerald I suppose you just wanted to be on your own and have a bit of peace and quiet, eh, Linda? Time to relax. Read a book. Have a few early nights.

Linda Yes. That *was* the idea ...

Gerald Got a nice room, have you?

Linda Oh, yes.

Gerald Private bath and all that?

Linda Oh, yes.

Gerald That's good. Only the best for my little girl. And don't worry about the expense. I'll pay for it. (*To Potter*) You sure she's got everything she wants up there, Potter?

Potter (*echoing Linda*) Oh, yes! (*Then hastily*) I think so ... !

Linda (*intervening, hastily*) Yes! A lovely view from the window! It looks out over the garden.

Gerald (*a little put-out*) Mine overlooks the car park ... Still, I'm glad. I always want the best for you. I'll pop up and have a look, shall I? (*He starts to go*)

Linda (*loudly*) No!!

Gerald (*surprised*) What?

Linda It's ... rather untidy.

Potter It shouldn't be. The maid cleaned it this morning ...

Linda (*snapping at Potter*) Well, it's untidy now! (*Then to Gerald*) There are ... things lying about.

Gerald That doesn't matter, Linda. It's only your old father. I'll just have a quick look—all right? (*He prepares to go up again*)

Linda No! No—I—I'll go and tidy it up a bit—*then* you can have a look.

Gerald (*giving in*) Oh, all right, then. But I can't think what you're making such a fuss about.

Potter (*quietly*) *I* can ... !

Linda I shan't be long. I'll let you know when it's all clear.

Gerald All *clear*?

Linda All tidy! (*She whispers urgently to Potter*) Don't let him know that I'm here with a man! (*Then to Gerald*) It's lovely to see you, Daddy. Yes. *What* a surprise!

She gives Potter a hectic look and races out DL

Gerald smiles happily, and returns to Potter

Gerald She's always been very fond of me ... (*Then sharply*) You never told me my daughter was here!

Potter I—I—I didn't know, did I? (*He backs away*)

Gerald (*pursuing him around the padded seat*) You didn't think it was a coincidence that you had two people booked in here with the same surname?

Potter (*blankly*) What?

Gerald Two Corbys!

Potter (*surprised*) Two Corbys *here*?

Gerald Me and my daughter!

Potter Oh, is that *her* name, too?

Gerald Well, she's unmarried, isn't she?

Potter (*uncertainly*) Is she?

Gerald Potter—if she was married, I'd have given her away, wouldn't I? *And* paid for the wedding! Surely you noticed that——?

Potter starts to flee towards the archway UR

Potter You mustn't speak to me! I've got work to do!

Gerald (*thoughtfully*) She must be using another name ... (*He picks up his orange juice from the garden table*)

Potter stops, uncertain

Potter What?

Gerald In the register! (*With sudden suspicion*) Why should she be using another name in the register? (*He sits on the padded seat*)

Potter (*miserably*) *I* don't know ... ! (*He starts to go again*)

Gerald She must have something to hide. ...

Potter stops again

Potter What?

Gerald Well, if she's got nothing to hide why would she be travelling incognito?

Potter You mustn't ask me! It's none of my business!

He darts out, quickly, before Gerald can stop him again

Gerald deep in thought, concentrates on his orange juice ...

In the bedroom ...

The door bursts open and Linda comes racing in, breathless

Linda Rodney! Quickly!

Rodney comes out of the bathroom. He is still wearing the short dressing-gown, but has now got his pyjama trousers on under it

Why are you wearing my dressing-gown?

Rodney I thought you were going to wait downstairs.

Linda I couldn't wait any longer.

He smiles, delightedly

Rodney Oh, good!

Linda locks the door. He smiles, optimistically

And you're locking the door! That's more like it! (*He leaps on to the bed and lies down, hopefully*)

Linda (*going to him*) No, Rodney! Not now!

Rodney No?

Linda No.

Rodney Then what have you come back for?

Linda Because you've got to go!

Rodney Yes, I know. The doctor wants to check my blood pressure. Make sure I'm fit for it. (*He laughs*)

Linda You can't stay here! (*She races about the room, collecting up some of his things*)

Rodney Can't I?

Linda Not in *this* room.

Rodney (*getting off the bed*) Don't say they've given us the wrong room?
Linda No. This is the right room.
Rodney Oh, good.
Linda But you can't stay in it.
Rodney Then it must be the *wrong* room.
Linda No. It's the right room. But *you*'ve got to go.
Rodney Yes—to the doctor. But I shan't be long.
Linda No! You mustn't come back here!
Rodney Well, where are we going to, then?
Linda We're not going anywhere.
Rodney But you said——!
Linda *I'm* staying here.
Rodney You said we had to go.
Linda No. *You*'ve got to go!
Rodney Even though this is the right room?
Linda It's the right room for *me*, but the wrong room for *you*.

Linda goes into the bathroom to collect his clothes, etc.

Rodney tries to work this out

Linda returns with his weekend bag and puts his things into it

Rodney You mean ... we aren't going to stay in the same room?
Linda Not any more.
Rodney But isn't that what we came here for?
Linda Yes.
Rodney That's what I thought.
Linda But now we can't.
Rodney So ... where shall *I* be sleeping?
Linda (*flustered*) I don't know! You'll have to find *another* room!
Rodney One room each?
Linda Yes.
Rodney Isn't that rather unusual?
Linda There's no time to argue!

He looks at the bed, sadly

Rodney It's a nice big bed ...
Linda I know.
Rodney You don't need that all to yourself.
Linda Yes, I do.
Rodney All of it?
Linda I like to stretch.
Rodney You'll be cold.
Linda I'll get a bottle.
Rodney But, Linda—if I stay in another room, won't people hear me creaking along the landing to *this* room?
Linda You won't be.
Rodney Of course I will!

Linda No.
Rodney Not just once?
Linda No.
Rodney If you're shy we'll turn the lights off.
Linda (*desperately*) Rodney—please go! (*She hands him his weekend bag*)

Rodney looks at the bag, bleakly

Rodney You've packed my bag.
Linda Yes. Everything's in there.

He smiles nervously

Rodney You are joking, aren't you?
Linda No, I'm not!
Rodney No, you're not ... Look—I can't go dressed like this!
Linda You can change downstairs. Please, Rodney! I can't explain now.
   Just go!

*She unlocks the door and opens it for him. He starts to go, dismally, but
hesitates in the doorway*

Rodney Shall I ... see you later?
Linda No! Whatever happens—you don't know me!
Rodney I don't?
Linda No.
Rodney Oh. Right. (*He is about to go, but hesitates again*) I hope you
   remembered to pack my toothbrush.

   He goes in a daze

Linda closes the door, relieved but fed up

Linda Oh, hell!

   She goes into the bathroom

In the pool area ...

Gerald is sipping his orange juice, thoughtfully

   *Rodney comes in, carrying his weekend bag. He wanders, gloomily, towards
   Gerald*

*Gerald looks up and sees Rodney in his pyjama bottoms and short feminine
dressing-gown*

Gerald I wouldn't go into the lounge dressed like that if I were you. Might
   give people funny ideas. (*He chuckles, then notices Rodney's gloomy face*)
   Something wrong?
Rodney Yes ... !
Gerald Don't say your girl-friend hasn't turned up?
Rodney (*gloomily*) Oh, she's turned up all right, but she won't let me in.
Gerald What?
Rodney She's locked me out of the bedroom!

Gerald Ah! That's why you're carrying your bag?
Rodney Yes . . .

Gerald begins to philosophize . . .

Gerald Funny blokes, women. Know what I mean? Unpredictable. Play hard to get sometimes. You want my advice? Well, of course you do! Don't you take no for an answer.
Rodney But she won't let me in!
Gerald All part of her game, isn't it?
Rodney Is it?
Gerald Oh, yes. She wants you to take her by storm.
Rodney That wasn't the impression *I* got . . . (*He sits on the sun lounger in despair*)
Gerald 'Course it wasn't! Because she's playing her game, isn't she? Women always play games.
Rodney Do they?
Gerald Oh, yes. So now it's all up to you.
Rodney Ah. I didn't know that.
Gerald You'll have to storm the battlements.
Rodney (*fed up*) How can I storm the battlements when the door's locked?
Gerald Use your initiative!
Rodney Initiative? I'll need a battering ram!
Gerald You'll just have to find another way to gain access.
Rodney Yes—but what?
Gerald That's up to you, son. You'll have to put on your thinking cap. (*He grins, encouragingly*)

But Rodney looks remarkably short of inspiration . . .

> *Potter comes bustling in* UR, *his clipboard under his arm, the burden of responsibility on his shoulders. He sees Rodney and Gerald together and reacts in alarm, fearing a confrontation that might disrupt the peace*

Potter Aaaah!
Gerald What's the matter?
Potter You're here!
Gerald Of course I'm here!
Potter And so is *he* . . .
Gerald Yes.
Potter You're *both* here.
Gerald Yes.
Potter Together.
Gerald Yes!
Potter (*apprehensively*) You haven't been . . . *talking* to each other, have you?
Gerald 'Course we've been talking to each other!

Potter shies like a nervous horse

Potter Ah! What about?

Gerald I was giving him a bit of advice.

Potter shies again

Potter Ah! What about?
Gerald About his girl-friend.

Potter shies again

Potter Ah! What girl-friend? (*To Rodney*) You haven't got a girl-friend!
Rodney I had before she locked me out ...
Potter No!
Rodney What?
Potter You're here on your own!
Rodney No, I'm not!
Potter Yes! *Yes!*
Gerald Potter, are you going mad?
Potter Very likely. What about the doctor?
Gerald Is *she* going mad, too?
Potter She will be soon. (*To Rodney, urgently*) You shouldn't be in here! You should be out there! The doctor's waiting for you! (*He pulls him to his feet and urges him on his way*)
Rodney (*fed up*) I'm not in the mood for the doctor ...
Potter But she's expecting you! You can't keep her waiting!
Rodney (*reluctantly*) Oh, all right ...
Potter If you go straight down the corridor you'll find——

Rodney joins in, impatiently

Potter } (*together*) —a green door marked "Private"—it's next to a blue
Rodney } door marked "Doctor"—that's where you'll find the doctor!

Rodney marches out through the archway with his bag

Potter is breathing heavily from all the excitement

Gerald You'd better calm down, Potter. If you go on like this you'll explode.

Sandra comes in DL. She is now wearing something she imagines to be sexy and provocative; a flowing, colourful, diaphanous number like something out of "The Arabian Nights". She does not see Potter as she glides across to Gerald

Potter moves down, gazing at her in moral horror

Sandra Aah ... there you are, Mr Corby!
Gerald (*seeing her*) Oh, my God ... !
Sandra I've been looking everywhere for you ... (*She parades herself in front of Gerald, speaking in a low dreamy, sexy voice*) I've ... changed ... my clothes, Mr Corby. Did you ... notice ... ? (*She pirouettes and sees Potter watching her in astonishment. She yells at him*) What are *you* doing here?

Potter You can't wander about dressed like that! This is a health farm, not a house of ill-repute! (*He bounces on the spot in moral frenzy*) Oh, please, please! Go and change ... !

Sandra I just have!

Potter Into something less ... less ...

Gerald It couldn't be *much* less.

Potter Less revealing! What will my other clients say if they see you like that? (*As he goes*) This is a respectable establishment!

Sandra (*giggling*) Not any more!

Potter disappears, hastily, UR

Gerald rises and moves towards the sun lounger

Gerald Now see what you've done! What's he going to think?

Sandra What does it matter?

Gerald He's the manager!

Sandra So what?

Gerald And he's a very moral manager. I don't want him getting hold of the wrong end of the stick. He might talk. Moral people always talk.

Sandra What about?

Gerald About other people's morals!

Sandra What does that matter? There's nobody here who knows you, is there?

Gerald No! No—of course not!

Sandra So what are you worrying about? Oh, Mr Corby ... (*She advances*)

Gerald Sandra! Please! (*He looks about, nervously*)

Sandra Don't you like it? (*She revolves sedately to show off her dress*)

Gerald stares at her in disbelief

Gerald You never carry on like this when we're in the office.

Sandra But we're not in the office now, Mr Corby.

Gerald I'm still your boss!

Sandra Even with your clothes off?

Gerald (*wearily*) Sandra—*please*—go away and leave me on my own ...

Sandra You wouldn't like it on your own, Mr Corby.

Gerald Look, Sandra——!

Sandra Why don't we have dinner together tonight?

Gerald You can hardly call it dinner! A thermos of soup and a bunch of grapes. (*He escapes further away* DL)

Sandra It wouldn't seem so bad if we shared it ...

Gerald No.

Sandra (*closing to him*) We could have it in *your* room.

Gerald No!

Sandra Then we can talk things over.

Gerald There's nothing to talk over!

Sandra I feel like a prisoner having dinner all on my own. Why don't I bring my tray along to your room, and then ... after you've had your soup ... I'll let you have some of my grapes.

Gerald (*appalled*) I don't want your grapes!
Sandra You might.
Gerald I won't!

Potter returns, holding a towelling robe up in front of his face so he cannot see her

Sandra *You* couldn't stay away long, could you?

He goes to her and holds out the towelling robe, carefully averting his eyes to prevent them settling on her scantily-clad figure

Potter Put this on please.
Sandra Oh, all right, Mr Potter. Anything you say. (*She slips into the robe*) You are an old spoilsport ...
Potter And now go and change. You were due for exercises half an hour ago.
Sandra I had exercises yesterday!
Potter Well, you're having them again today!

He gives her a hefty push which almost sends her flying

Sandra Don't go away, Mr Corby. I'll be back!

She winks at Gerald and goes out to the bedrooms

Potter looks at Gerald with a critical eye. Gerald tries to retain his innocence

Gerald It's not as bad as it looks, Potter.
Potter Oh, I *hope* not, sir. The pillars of morality already appear to be trembling.
Gerald You needn't worry about *my* morals! I'm hardly likely to chase after my own secretary, am I?
Potter (*appalled*) She's not your ... *secretary*?
Gerald Yes.
Potter Oh, no ... ! (*He sinks his face into his hand in despair*)
Gerald (*defensively*) *I* didn't know she was going to be here!

Potter smiles, wanly

Potter You can hardly expect anyone to believe that, sir. A man travelling with his secretary is certain to raise eyebrows.
Gerald Don't be potty, Potter!

He starts to go towards the archway DL

Potter shies again like a nervous horse

Potter Ah! Where are you going, sir?

Gerald stops and looks at him in surprise

Gerald What's it got to do with you? I'm going to find my daughter.

Potter shies again

Potter Ah! What?!

Gerald Well, she must have tidied up her room by now. I want to see what it's like. (*He continues on his way*) *And* I want to know why she's travelling incognito ...

He marches out with a determined tread ...

Potter looks alarmed and steps over the sun lounger to call after him, anxiously

Potter Well, don't stay too long!

Rodney returns, still carrying his weekend bag

Potter turns, sees him, shies nervously, and goes quickly to him, stepping over the sun lounger again as he does so

Ah! You can't have finished with the doctor yet!
Rodney I couldn't find her!
Potter Oh, good!
Rodney What?
Potter Follow me! (*He leads the way*) I'll show you to the green door marked "Private"——

Rodney joins in, wearily

Potter } (*together*) —it's next to a blue door marked "Doctor"—that's
Rodney }   where you'll find the doctor ...

They disappear through the archway UR

In the bedroom ...

As Potter and Rodney go, there is a knock at the bedroom door

Linda comes in from the bathroom, alarmed. She is now wearing a short, towelling robe

She calls out

Linda Go away! You can't come in!

Another knock at the door. She goes across to hiss, urgently, at the door

I told you to go away! You're not to come back in!
Gerald (*off*) It's only me, Linda!
Linda Oh, my God ... ! (*She unlocks the door and opens it*)

Gerald pops his head in, smiling broadly

(*A little surprised*) Daddy! It's you! Come on in.

Gerald comes in. Linda looks quickly out of the door to make sure there is no sign of Rodney, then closes the door and leans against it, relieved

Gerald is looking about the room, heavily suspicious

Gerald Got the place all tidied up, then?

Linda Yes.

Gerald Cleared away all the rubbish?

Linda I hope so ... !

Gerald Very nice room.

Linda Yes.

Gerald (*eyeing it suspiciously*) Nice big bed ...

Linda Yes.

Gerald (*sulking*) I've only got a single bed in *my* room ...

Linda (*innocently*) Really?

Gerald How long ago did you book?

Linda Last week.

Gerald I booked a month ago! And all *I* got was a single bed overlooking the car park. (*He sulks a little*)

Linda Well, did you *ask* for a double?

Gerald No, of course not. Did *you*?

Linda (*hastily*) Ah! No! But they ... they hadn't got a single left. So I had to have a double.

Gerald's mercenary nature asserts itself

Gerald You're not *paying* for a double, are you?

Linda Er ... no. I—I don't suppose so ...

Gerald heads for the telephone

Gerald I'll have a word with them. They can't charge you for a double if you only asked for a single. (*He lifts the receiver*)

Linda (*alarmed*) No! Please, Daddy——!

Gerald I'll get it sorted out.

Linda But it doesn't matter—really! (*She replaces the receiver*)

Gerald 'Course it matters—I'm paying! (*He lifts the receiver again*)

Linda No! (*She replaces the receiver again*) You see—I ... I *may* have booked a double.

Gerald What?!

Linda By mistake!

Gerald Well, they can't charge you extra if you made a mistake. (*He lifts the receiver*)

Linda No! (*She replaces the receiver*)

Gerald (*with a shrug*) All right, Linda. If that's what you want. Only trying to help my little girl. (*He kisses her, briefly, and wanders away, looking about*) Who did you think I was, then?

Linda Sorry?

Gerald When I knocked at the door.

Linda Oh ... er ... nobody.

Gerald You said, "Go away, you can't come back in" to *nobody*?

Linda The chambermaid! She keeps trying to get into the bedroom.

Gerald What for?

Linda Well ... to see to things.

Gerald (*smiling*) That's what she's paid for, to see to things.

Linda But she *keeps* trying to see to them!

Gerald Well, if you let her see to them, she'll have seen to them, won't she? Then she won't have to see to them again.

Linda But I don't want her to see to them! Not *now*! It's too early. You can't see to things when the sun's still shining—and it is, you see?—look!—out there!—the sun's shining!

Gerald ambles across to look out of the window

Gerald So it is! (*He studies the view*) Oh, yes. You *have* got a nice view of the garden, haven't you? (*Gloomily*) My room looks over the car park . . .

Linda (*going to him*) Well, did you *ask* for a view of the garden?

Gerald No, of course not. Did *you*?

Linda (*hastily*) No! I . . . I don't think so.

Gerald Then they can't charge you for it. I'll have a word with them. (*He trots off towards the phone again*)

Linda No, Daddy!

She pursues him and they have a small race, but Gerald gets there first and lifts the receiver. They struggle for possession

I don't want any fuss—really!

She pulls the receiver from him, abruptly, and replaces it. He looks at her, suspiciously

Gerald You haven't got something to hide, have you?

Linda (*nervously*) W-what?

Gerald Some dark secret . . . ?

Linda N—no, no—of course not. . . . (*She moves away*)

Gerald Then why are you staying here . . . incognito?

Linda Sorry?

Gerald Under an assumed name!

Linda Yes. I know what the *word* means. I just don't know what *you* mean.

Gerald (*going to her, ponderously*) There's only one Corby in the register . . .

Linda Is there?

Gerald And that's *me*.

Linda Ah! Yes! Well, I . . . I didn't want anyone to know I was here.

Gerald Why not?

Linda Because I came here for a bit of . . .

Gerald A bit of what?

Linda Peace and quiet!

She sits, wearily, in the armchair, apparently exhausted and overdoes it a bit

I've been working so hard lately . . .

Gerald Have you?

Linda You know I have!

Gerald Yes—yes, of course!

Linda Daddy, I don't think you realize quite how hard I *have* been working . . .

Gerald feels guilty and coos, sympathetically

Gerald Yes. Of *course* you have . . .
Linda I just needed to get away . . . alone.
Gerald Yes. Of *course* you did . . .
Linda And I couldn't have peace and quiet if people were ringing me up all the time, could I? So I thought it would be safer just to call myself . . . (*as if it was an original idea*) . . . Smith!

Gerald beams at her, proudly, marvelling at her brilliance

Gerald Of course! What a good idea!
Linda (*pouting, sadly*) And *you* thought I had something to hide . . .
Gerald Well, I——
Linda Oh, Daddy! How *could* you?

He looks suitably shamefaced and gives her a quick kiss

Gerald Yes, yes, I—I'm sorry. I should have known better. (*He escapes and looks about with unconcealed envy*) This really is nice. Can I look at your bathroom?
Linda You must have seen a bathroom before.
Gerald (*grimly*) I want to see if it's better than mine . . .

He goes into the bathroom

Linda leaps up and races across to the main door, opens it and looks out, furtively, into the corridor to make sure that Rodney is not about

Lights out in the bedroom

In the pool area . . .

Rodney walks in from the archway UR. *He no longer has his weekend bag. He looks about to see that all is clear and then starts to hasten off in the direction of the bedrooms*

Potter comes racing in, carrying the register, pursuing Rodney

Potter Aah!
Rodney (*jumping a mile*) Aah!
Potter Where are *you* going?
Rodney Upstairs.
Potter You can't do that!
Rodney I thought I'd just see if I'm still locked out.
Potter You are!
Rodney She might have changed her mind. (*He starts to go again*)
Potter She hasn't! (*He urges Rodney on his way*) Why don't you go and sit in the garden? It's a beautiful garden so why don't you go and sit in it? And if you feel a bit lonely you can have a nice chat with the gardener. *He's* out there. I'll send out a pot of tea for two.

He pushes Rodney, who goes flying out through the archway UR. *Potter goes racing out at high speed towards the bedrooms, jumping across the sun lounger as he goes*

Lights up in the bedroom ...

Linda comes back into the room and closes the door as Gerald comes out of the bathroom holding up a man's pyjama jacket

Gerald Linda ... ?
Linda Yes?
Gerald What the hell's this?

Linda sees it and jumps

Linda Aah! It ... it looks like a pyjama jacket.
Gerald It *is* a pyjama jacket. A *man*'s pyjama jacket!
Linda W-where did you find it?
Gerald In there! Hanging up behind the door! What's a man's pyjama jacket doing hanging up in your bathroom?
Linda He must have left it behind.
Gerald What?!
Linda The last guest! When he went. He was probably in a hurry and left it behind.
Gerald Why aren't there any trousers?
Linda Perhaps he doesn't *wear* trousers.
Gerald Funny sort of man who'd come to a health farm without his pyjama trousers.
Linda He might have been a Scotsman. They don't always wear trousers. They quite often wear kilts.
Gerald Not in bed!
Linda They might if they're drunk.

There is a knock at the door. Linda looks alarmed. Gerald hastily hides the pyjama jacket in the armchair

Oh, my God ... !
Gerald Who can that be? (*He starts to go*)
Linda No!—I'll go! It might be the chambermaid again. (*She calls out, her face close to the door*) My *father* wants to know who it is!

Gerald looks surprised at this

Potter (*off*) It's me—Potter!
Linda (*to Gerald, relieved*) It's Potter!

She opens the door. Potter is there

Gerald Ah—Potter! Come on in. Just the man I want to see.
Potter (*going to Gerald*) It's time for your sauna, sir!
Gerald (*glancing at his watch*) Don't be daft. Half an hour yet. (*He puts his arm around Potter's shoulders*) I just want to get a couple of things straight. All right?
Potter (*anxiously*) Couldn't we talk in my office——? (*He starts to go*)

Gerald grabs his arm and pulls him back again

Gerald It won't take a minute. Now, the thing is—my daughter only booked a *single* room.

Potter But this is Number Ten. And Number Ten is a double room. (*He consults the register*) Yes! Number Ten—double! It says so here. No doubt about it.

He snaps the register shut. It emits a small cloud of dust, making him splutter a little

Gerald Ah! But she only asked for a single.
Potter (*to Linda*) Did you?
Linda Yes! I did! But all the single rooms were occupied. (*Nodding in time to the words*) Surely you *remember*?
Potter (*shaking his head in time to the words*) No, I don't remember!
Linda (*nodding in time*) Yes, you do remember! (*She stares at him, appealing desperately*)
Potter (*reluctantly*) Oh, very well . . . ! (*Nodding in time*) Yes, I do remember! (*He turns to Gerald and continues nodding*) Yes, I do remember——!
Gerald Are you trying to tell me that all the single rooms were occupied?
Potter Yes. So your daughter had to have a double . . .
Gerald Which, of course, she will not be paying for!
Potter I beg your pardon?
Gerald You can't expect my daughter to pay for a double when all she wanted was a single.

Potter dives into the register again

Potter Let's have a look, shall we? See if there's a note in here about non-payment of a double when occupied as a single . . .
Gerald There doesn't need to be a note!
Potter That's what I thought . . . !

He snaps the register shut, emitting another puff of dust. Again he splutters

Gerald (*going to the window*) Now come over here!
Potter Sorry?
Gerald Come and look at this!

Potter exchanges a bewildered look with Linda, then trots across to join Gerald at the window. Gerald nods, indicating something outside

You see that out there?
Potter (*peering out*) What?
Gerald The view! The view of the bloody garden!
Potter (*enthusiastically*) Oh, yes! It's lovely, isn't it, sir? Much better than the car park . . .
Gerald Well, she's not paying for *that*, either!
Potter The car park?
Gerald The view! (*Ponderously*) She's not . . . paying . . . for the bloody view!
Potter Oh, I think the view comes with the room. I don't think you can have the room without the view. Let's see what it says here—(*He opens the register again*)
Gerald (*losing his cool*) Never mind what it says there!

Gerald snaps the register shut this time. A bigger cloud of dust. And again poor Potter splutters

Potter Oh, dear. I shall be coughing all night after this. And I never can find my linctus ...
Gerald Right! Let's make a note of that in the register.

He opens the register and helps himself to the pen from Potter's pocket. Linda looks alarmed and grabs Potter's arm

Linda (*whispering, urgently*) Don't let him look at that ... !
Potter What?
Linda The register ... ! (*But it is too late*)
Gerald Wait a minute! What's this? It says here—"Room Ten—Mr and Mrs Smith"! (*He looks up at them*) "Mr and Mrs"?
Linda Ah! Er—you can explain that, can't you, Mr Potter?
Potter No.
Linda Yes!
Potter No-o-o ... !
Linda (*quietly*) *Please*, Potter ... !
Gerald Well, Potter?

Potter looks at Linda. She nods, encouragingly, and pushes him towards Gerald

Potter Well, it's ... it's ... for the records.
Gerald What records?

Potter looks at Linda again. She nods, desperately, and pushes him towards Gerald again. Potter succumbs, suffering at allowing himself to be a party to such subterfuge

Potter Well, you see ... (*he takes a deep breath and keeps talking steadily and without pause*)—they're very fond of records at Head Office and after all this is a double room although on this occasion occupied by a single client due to lack of availability of single accommodation but to Head Office it is still designated as a double and therefore double meaning two Head Office will expect two names to be entered in the register for Number Ten it being a double although as we all know on this particular occasion your daughter Miss Corby is the sole occupant thereof.

Linda smiles, gratefully. Gerald gazes at Potter, astonished by this speedy exposition

Gerald I beg your pardon?
Potter I'm not saying all *that* again ... !
Linda I don't know what Mr Potter must think of you, Daddy. All these questions. (*Going to him*) Surely you aren't suspicious of your own daughter?
Gerald No—no, of course not. (*He kisses her quickly*) But I was bound to wonder, wasn't I? When I found ... *what* I found ... in the bathroom.
Potter (*to Linda*) What *have* you left lying about?

Gerald I mean—what was I supposed to think? Look at this! (*He picks up the pyjama jacket and holds it aloft like a flag*) A man's pyjama jacket!

Potter stares at the pyjama jacket in horror

You still haven't explained how the hell this came to be here!

A dreadful pause. Then Linda thinks of a way out

Linda It . . . it belongs to Mr Potter.

Potter and Gerald react

Potter } (*together*) What?
Gerald }

Gerald glares at Potter

Gerald *Yours*?!
Potter No!
Linda Yes!
Potter No! I've never seen it before!
Linda Yes, you have! Don't you remember? You left it in here.
Gerald (*apoplectic*) You left your pyjama jacket in my daughter's bedroom?
Potter No!
Linda Of course he did!
Gerald Then why's he saying "no"?
Linda Well, he's bound to say no *now*, isn't he?
Gerald Is he? (*To Potter*) Have you got something to hide?
Potter No! I'm a very moral man!
Gerald But my daughter says you left your pyjama tops in her bedroom.
Potter Well, she's wrong!
Gerald Are you calling my only daughter a liar?
Potter No, but——
Gerald So you *did* leave this here?
Potter No!
Linda Yes!
Gerald You took off your pyjama jacket in my daughter's bedroom?
Linda Don't be silly, Daddy. He wasn't wearing it at the time.
Gerald He wasn't?
Linda Of course not.
Potter Thank God for that . . . !
Gerald Well, I hope you were wearing the *other* half!
Potter What other half?
Gerald The *bottom* half!
Linda No. He wasn't wearing that, either.
Gerald He wasn't?!
Potter I wasn't?!
Linda Of course not.
Gerald Then what *was* he wearing?
Linda He was dressed like he is now.
Gerald Fully-clothed?

Linda Of course.

Potter Oh, that *is* a relief. . . .

Gerald Then why did he leave his pyjama tops in here?

Linda I *told* him he could.

Gerald What the hell for?

Linda He'd lost a button off the jacket so I said I'd sew it back on for him.

Gerald Why couldn't he sew it on himself?

Linda Daddy, you could hardly expect the manager of a health farm to sew on his own buttons! So *I* said I'd do it *for* him.

She takes the pyjama jacket from Gerald and thrusts it into Potter's hands

There you are, Mr Potter. The button's back on again.

Potter (*gazing at it, mournfully*) Yes. You'd think it had never been off . . .

Gerald (*thoughtfully*) But, Linda—how the hell did you know he'd lost a button off his pyjamas in the first place?

But before Linda has to reply Rodney starts to climb in through the bedroom window! He is still wearing pyjama trousers and the rather feminine dressing-gown

They all look at the intruder in astonishment. Rodney is inside before he straightens up and sees not only Linda (as he expected) but also Potter and Gerald. He is deeply embarrassed

Quite a pause. Nobody knows what to say. Then . . .

Potter (*puzzled*) Why is he coming in through the window?

Linda realizes that she must warn Rodney and calls out to her father, dramatically

Linda Oh, *Daddy*!

Rodney (*appalled*) D—d—daddy . . . ?

Linda There's a burglar!

Gerald He's not a burglar.

Linda Oh, *Daddy*! What's he doing in my bedroom?

Gerald I'm just going to ask him. (*He goes towards Rodney*)

Rodney cowers as Gerald approaches

Potter Oh, dear. I feel the pillars of morality are moving again. . . .

Gerald (*to Rodney*) What the hell are you doing in *here*?

Rodney I . . . I've come to clean the windows.

Gerald *You're* not a window-cleaner!

Rodney Yes, I am!

Potter (*quietly, to Linda*) Is he?

Linda Yes—he *is*!

Potter No wonder he seems so at home on a ladder . . .

Gerald (*chuckling*) You'd be a funny sort of window-cleaner arriving without a bucket!

Rodney I knew I'd forgotten something. (*He starts to go out of the window again*)

Gerald Where are you going?

Rodney To get my bucket. I must have left it at the bottom of the ladder.

Gerald (*laughing*) No, no! Wait a minute!

Rodney stops again, nervously

Gerald (*confidentially*) Whatever made you come into *this* room?

Rodney I told you—I'm here to clean the windows! (*He starts to sing*) "I go cleaning windows to earn an honest bob, For a nosey-parker it's an interesting job——"

Gerald Don't be daft! I *know* what you're doing, don't I?

Rodney Do you?

Gerald You're storming the battlements!

Linda (*to Potter*) What's he talking about?

Potter Don't ask me! I've been the manager here for five years and I've never known anyone come in through a window and sing a song before . . .

Rodney I'll just go and get my bucket. (*He starts to go again*)

Gerald You are an idiot!

Rodney Yes. I know!

Gerald The intention was good, son. Finding a ladder and all that.

Rodney (*with a nervous smile*) I borrowed it from the gardener. He'd been cutting back the ivy . . .

Gerald Full marks! E for Effort. Only thing is—(*he leans forward, confidentially*)—you came into the wrong room, didn't you?

Rodney Did I?

Gerald I can understand your mistake.

Rodney Can you?

Gerald I expect all the windows look alike from outside. In the heat of the moment—passion running high—difficult to pinpoint the right room, eh?

Rodney Well . . . yes, it was rather difficult . . .

Gerald So if I were you—you don't mind me making a suggestion?

Rodney No, no—please. I'm glad of your help.

Potter (*to Linda*) What's he talking about?

Linda Don't ask me!

Gerald I think you should go back down the ladder——

Rodney Good idea! I'll go *now*——

Gerald Hang on!

Rodney (*hesitating*) Not yet?

Gerald In a minute.

Rodney Right. No hurry.

Gerald Go down the ladder——

Rodney Yes?

Gerald (*chuckling*) Try not to put your foot in the bucket!

Rodney (*laughing also*) I'll be careful.

Gerald Move the ladder.

Rodney Move it. Yes.

Gerald Along a bit.

Rodney Which way?

Gerald That's up to you.
Rodney Right.
Gerald Along to *your* room.
Rodney How do I know which that is?
Gerald Well, one thing's for sure.
Rodney What's that?
Gerald (*laughing*) It's not *this* one!
Rodney No! It certainly isn't! (*He laughs also, but rather nervously*)
Gerald I should try the one next door.
Rodney Good idea. Can I go now?
Gerald Why not?
Rodney Thank goodness for that . . . ! (*He starts to go again*)
Gerald Wait a minute!

Rodney stops, nervously

Rodney I *thought* things were going too smoothly . . .
Linda (*loudly, going to them*) Don't stop him!!

They look at her in surprise

Gerald What?
Linda He was just going!
Gerald Yes, I know, but——
Linda I don't want a burglar in my bedroom!
Gerald But he's not a burglar.
Linda (*to Rodney, urgently*) Go on! You can't stay here!
Rodney I'm *trying* to go . . . !
Potter Yes, he is!
Gerald Just a minute!

Rodney stops, half-way out of the window. Linda panics

Linda Don't stop him now!
Gerald I'm a bit puzzled about something . . .
Linda No, you're not! Everything's perfectly clear! (*To Rodney, desperately*) Go *on*!
Gerald I know he's not a burglar . . .
Linda Yes, he is!
Gerald And I know he's not a window-cleaner . . .
Potter } (*together*) Yes, he *is*!
Linda }
Gerald But what I don't know . . . is how he comes to be wearing the bottom half of *his* pyjamas! (*Indicating Potter*)

Rodney looks at Potter, who is still holding the pyjama jacket. And Potter looks at Rodney. Then they both look down at their respective garments

Linda Mr Potter lent them to him!
Potter No, I didn't! (*He hastily puts down the pyjama jacket*)
Linda Of course you did!
Gerald (*apoplectic*) You lent him your pyjama bottoms?!

Potter sees Linda's desperate, appealing look and relents

Potter Apparently ...
Gerald Why?
Potter He hadn't got any of his own.
Gerald (*to Rodney*) You came to this place without your pyjama bottoms?
Rodney Yes.
Gerald Why?
Rodney I didn't think I was going to need them.
Gerald What?!
Linda I expect he thought they'd be provided.
Gerald (*pompously*) *I* brought *my* pyjama bottoms.
Potter Well, next time you can lend him *yours* ... !
Gerald I can't think why you were wearing pyjama bottoms in the first place.
Rodney It's this dressing-gown. It's a bit short.
Potter Yes, it is! Far too short!
Gerald You'd better go and get your trousers on.
Rodney Good idea! (*He starts to go*)
Gerald So give Mr Potter back his bottoms.
Rodney What? Oh—yes. Right.

Deeply embarrassed, Rodney takes off his pyjama bottoms and gives them to Linda

There you are.

Linda passes them to Potter

Thank you, Mr Potter.
Potter It's all part of the service ... (*He rolls the pyjama bottoms into a ball*)
Rodney (*to Gerald*) Er ... is it all right if I carry on now?
Gerald Yes, of course. So sorry. You want to get away, don't you?
Rodney I certainly do ... !
Gerald Right, then—you go and storm the battlements next door! (*He laughs*)
Rodney Right. (*He gets out of the window*)
Potter (*alarmed*) What?!

Rodney starts to go down the ladder, but slips and disappears, abruptly

Rodney (*off*) Aaaah!

They all move, instinctively, towards the window in alarm

All Ooooooh!

Rodney's face reappears, sheepishly

Rodney I missed a couple of rungs.

He smiles nervously, and goes down the ladder more carefully this time. He disappears

Gerald Poor chap. He's in a bit of a state.
Potter (*moving away*) He's not the only one ... !
Linda Have you met him before, then, Daddy?
Gerald Yes. Downstairs. We had quite a chat.
Linda Oh, I see ... (*She moves to Potter, helplessly*)
Gerald He came here with a girl, you know. (*He looks out of the window*)
You all right, Rodney? (*He chuckles, peering down at Rodney*)
Potter (*whispering to Linda*) I didn't think he knew about you.
Linda (*whispering also*) He doesn't!
Potter You mean there's *another* girl?
Linda No. But *he* doesn't know that.

Gerald withdraws his head from outside the window, trying to control his laughter

Gerald Oh, dear, Oh dear ... !
Linda (*going to him in wide-eyed innocence*) Daddy, if that man's here with a girl-friend, why is he outside my window climbing up a ladder?
Gerald (*laughing*) Because she's locked him out of their room! (*He sits in the armchair, helpless with mirth*)
Linda She *hasn't*!
Gerald So I gave him a bit of advice. I told him to storm the battlements! But he picked the wrong room! (*He laughs, uproariously*)
Potter And now he's going to try the room next door?
Gerald Yes!
Potter Oh, my God ... ! (*He starts to go*)
Gerald Where are *you* going?
Potter Next door—before somebody *else* gets a nasty surprise! (*He continues on his way and opens the door*)
Gerald Well, don't forget your pyjamas!
Potter What? Oh—yes! Oh, dear ...

He exchanges a look with Linda, and stumbles out in despair with the pyjamas

Gerald (*glancing at his watch*) Right! I'd better go and have my sauna. (*He gets up and starts to go*)
Linda *I* feel as if I've already *had* one. ...
Gerald Perhaps I'll see you later?
Linda Yes. I'll keep an eye out for you ...
Gerald (*hesitating at the door*) It's a funny thing, you know ...
Linda Oh?
Gerald That dressing-gown thing he was wearing ...
Linda Yes?
Gerald I could have sworn I've seen it somewhere before. ...

He goes, deep in thought, and closes the door behind him

Linda falls straight backwards on to the bed, exhausted and relieved

In the pool area ...

Potter comes in, carrying the pyjamas, and meets Sandra, who is entering from the archway UR. *She is now wearing shorts and a shirt from the exercise class*

Sandra Have you seen him anywhere?

Potter shies, nervously

Potter Ah! What?
Sandra I'm looking for Mr Corby. I've got a nice surprise for him.
Potter Oh, no—no, miss—no more surprises, I beg of you ...
Sandra Have you seen him anywhere?
Potter Yes, I have—but you keep away from him! You can't have hanky-panky on a health farm. (*He starts to go*)
Sandra Mr Potter——?

Potter hesitates

Potter Yes?
Sandra Why are you walking about with a pair of gentleman's pyjamas?

Potter looks down at the pyjamas, having forgotten about them

Potter I'm looking after them for a friend.

He hastens off through the archway UR

Sandra laughs, and settles herself down on the garden seat to wait for Gerald

In the bedroom ...

A face rises into view outside the window as Rodney looks in, sees Linda is alone and taps on the glass

Linda sees him

Linda Rodney!

She races across to the door, locks it and runs to the open window

Rodney Have they all gone?
Linda Yes. You can come in.

Rodney climbs in through the bedroom window, breathless

Are you all right?
Rodney I am *now* ...

They embrace

In the pool area ...

Gerald walks in, heading for the sauna

Sandra rises and meets him with a big smile. Gerald looks at her, apprehensively

The dialogue in both scenes now interlocks

Sandra I've been looking for you ...
Gerald Go away!
Rodney You never said your father was here.
Sandra Mr Potter's found you a better bedroom.
Linda Well, I didn't *know*, did I?
Gerald What?
Rodney You said we'd be safe.
Sandra There's been a cancellation.
Linda That's what I thought.
Gerald What are you talking about?
Sandra So now you won't be over the car park.
Rodney What will he say if he finds you here with me?
Gerald That *is* good news!
Linda He *mustn't* find us!
Rodney What are we going to do, then?
Sandra You can move in now if you like.
Gerald Did Potter say which room it was?
Sandra Number Fourteen.
Rodney I'm getting out of here!
Linda You can't!
Gerald I'll move as soon as I've had my sauna.
Rodney What?
Sandra I'll come and help you.
Linda You haven't got any clothes on.
Gerald No, you won't!
Rodney Oh, my God! Where are they?
Linda In your suitcase.
Gerald There's something I want to ask you——
Rodney Where's my suitcase?
Sandra The answer to that is "yes"!
Linda You left it downstairs.
Gerald I want you to do something for me.
Rodney You mean I've got to go down there dressed in *this* again?
Sandra Anything you like ...
Linda But you don't have to rush!
Rodney Oh, yes, I do!
Gerald Something unexpected has cropped up——
Linda Haven't you noticed anything?
Sandra Yes—*me*!
Rodney What?
Linda We're on our own.
Gerald So I want *you* to keep out of sight.
Sandra I'll be very subtle ...
Linda And the door's locked ...
Sandra Nobody will suspect.
Gerald There's nothing *to* suspect!
Rodney Are you sure?
Linda Positive.

Sandra There soon *will* be!
Linda So don't let's waste any more time.
Gerald You stay away from me!

Gerald hastens into the steam bath

Linda Oh, darling—!

Linda and Rodney kiss each other

Sandra —you're going to have *such* a lovely surprise in Number Fourteen . . .!

Sandra runs out after Gerald

Marion walks in from the archway UR. *She is a highly attractive, well-dressed, sophisticated woman in her mid-forties. Potter is fluttering along behind her, still carrying the pyjamas*

Marion Why are you following me about waving your pyjamas in the air?
Potter They're not my pyjamas!
Marion Then whose pyjamas are they?
Potter I don't know!
Marion Then you'd better give them to the manager.
Potter I *am* the manager!
Marion Good. Then perhaps you can help me. I'm Mrs Corby. I'm looking for my husband.

Linda and Rodney collapse onto the bed, giggling happily

At the same time, the door to the steam bath bursts open and Gerald comes running out, hotly pursued by Sandra. Potter hastily grabs Marion and clutches her to his chest. She struggles, valiantly

Gerald and Sandra race across below Potter and Marion, without seeing them, and disappear out the other side

Marion escapes from Potter's clutches, appalled. She pushes him away, abruptly, and looks in the direction of the departing Gerald. Potter falls back on to the sun lounger in disarray, the picture of misery

Black-out

CURTAIN

ACT II

The same. A few minutes later

In the bedroom, Linda and Rodney are lying on the bed, kissing each other

After a moment, Rodney extricates himself

Rodney It's no good. I can't concentrate.
Linda (*a little put out*) Why not?
Rodney Your father might come in!
Linda He can't. The door's locked.
Rodney The *window*'s open! (*He gets off the bed*) I'm going to get my clothes and go home. (*He goes to the window and starts to climb out*)
Linda Oh, Rodney ...!

He stops

Rodney Well, I didn't think it was going to be like this ...

Linda gets off the bed and runs to him

Linda I'm sorry. It's all my fault. Next time we'll go to the *Holiday Inn*.
Rodney If there *is* a next time ...
Linda (*upset*) What ...?
Rodney Well, I don't know if my nerves would stand a second attempt. (*He starts to go down the ladder*)
Linda Rodney!

He stops

Goodbye, then ... (*She kisses him, gently*)
Rodney Goodbye ... (*He moves to go*)
Linda Rodney!

He stops again

Goodbye ... (*She kisses him again*)
Rodney Goodbye ...

He starts to disappear down the ladder outside

Linda Rodney!

He stops, only the top of his head visible through the window

I do love you ...

She kisses the top of his head, then taps it lightly. The head disappears out of sight down the ladder

Oh hell!

She goes out into the bathroom, closing the door behind her

In the pool area ...

Gerald comes in DL, *looking about, furtively, for Sandra. At the same time, Potter comes in from the archway* UR, *also looking about. They back towards each other, both unaware of the other's presence. They sit on opposite sides of the sun lounger and collide, back-to-back, and react in surprise*

Gerald } (*together*) Ah! (*They leap to their feet*)
Potter

Gerald Have you seen her anywhere?

Potter Which one, sir?

Gerald What?

Potter (*piously*) I hope you're looking for the right one ...

Gerald Is there *more* than one?

Potter Didn't you see the other one?

Gerald What other one?

Potter Standing here! Just now!

Gerald I couldn't see *anything* with Sandra after me!

Potter Well, there *was* one.

Gerald In here?

Potter She *was* in here. But now she's out there. Having a cup of tea in the garden. That's why I'm looking for you. I didn't want her to see you if the other one was still about. I wouldn't want you to get off on the wrong foot with *this* one.

Gerald Which one?

Potter The one having tea. She's just arrived.

Gerald What's that got to do with me?

Potter She's come to see you!

Gerald Has she?

Potter Yes. (*He smiles happily*) So that's good news, isn't it, sir?

Gerald Is it?

Potter Yes. And I'm so glad!

Gerald You?

Potter Yes.

Gerald Why?

Potter Because she seems to have arrived just in time to restore the temporarily tottering pillars of respectability.

Gerald What are you talking about?

Potter Your *wife* sir!

Gerald What wife?

Potter Don't tell me you haven't got a wife?

Gerald Yes. But she's at home.

Potter Not any more. She's here. Out there.

Gerald Having tea?

Potter Exactly.

Gerald She didn't see Sandra chasing me, did she?

Potter No. I was embracing her at the time.

Gerald What?!

Potter To stop her seeing you and Sandra!

Gerald Oh, well done, Potter! I wouldn't like her to get the wrong impression. What's she doing here anyway? She never said she was coming.

Potter (*smiling, benignly*) I knew you'd be pleased to see her!

Gerald Did you?

Potter And so am I!

Gerald You?

Potter Yes.

Gerald Why?

Potter Because I'm a manager who's very keen on morals.

Gerald And quite right, too. So whatever happens—keep Sandra out of the way! I don't want my wife thinking the worst.

Potter I'll do my best, sir.

Gerald Oh, and Potter——

Potter Yes?

Gerald (*shaking Potter's hand, vigorously*) Thank you! I'm very pleased!

Potter (*moved almost to tears*) Aah—about your wife. I *knew* you would be . . .

Gerald No, no. About my room.

Potter Pleased about your room? I thought you didn't like it.

Gerald I didn't like the *old* one, but I shall like *this* one.

Potter Which one?

Gerald The new one.

Potter What?

Gerald Look—I mustn't hang about here in case Sandra spots me—so when my wife's finished her tea, send her up to Number Fourteen.

Potter (*puzzled*) Number Fourteen?

Gerald That's where I'll be.

Potter You can't go in Number Fourteen!

Gerald Don't be daft, Potter! You've just put me in there!

Potter In Number Fourteen?

Gerald Yes! And I'm very grateful!

Gerald goes marching out to the bedrooms

Potter is left bewildered as . . .

Marion comes in from the garden with her cup of tea

Marion I've just seen a man climbing down a ladder without any trousers on.

Potter That'll be the window-cleaner.

Marion Without his trousers?

Potter He always takes them off in the hot weather.

Marion How very exciting . . . Now—where shall I find him?

Potter The window-cleaner?

Marion My husband! What's the number of his room?

Potter Ah—er—I'm not sure . . .

Marion I thought you were the manager?

Potter I am, but I'm not managing very well! (*He takes the spoon from her saucer and stirs her tea, briskly*)

Marion You must know which room he's in!

Potter (*quietly*) I wish I didn't . . . ! Now, look—(*he grabs her shoulders*)

Marion You're embracing me again!

Potter (*pushing her down on to the seat*) You stay here! I'll go and warn him—er—*find* him!—and bring him to you—*here*—*now*!

Marion Oh, very well. But don't keep embracing me.

Potter runs out to the bedrooms

Marion shrugs, resignedly, and settles with her tea to wait

> *Rodney comes in from the garden, looking about, but not seeing Marion. As he reaches the sun lounger, she sees a familiar pair of legs*

I think I've seen those legs before . . .

Rodney (*jumping, nervously*) What?!

Marion Were they at the top of a ladder just now?

Rodney Ah—yes. Er . . . (*He tries to make the dressing-gown longer by bending his knees*)

Marion So *you're* the one who takes off his trousers in the hot weather?

Rodney Sorry?

Marion You are a window-cleaner?

Rodney Ah—yes. But not now. Now I'm on holiday.

Marion So why were you up a ladder?

Rodney I . . . I couldn't get into my bedroom. The door was locked and I couldn't find my key.

Marion You should have asked Mr Potter for a spare one.

Rodney Well, by then I'd found this ladder . . .

Marion I see. (*She looks at him, admiringly*) Well, you *do* look pretty.

Rodney glances, embarrassed, at his female dressing-gown

Rodney It's not mine.

Marion I didn't mean the dressing-gown . . .

He shifts, awkwardly, under her direct look

Rodney I . . . I *was* wearing pyjama bottoms.

Marion (*intrigued*) Were you?

Rodney Oh, yes.

Marion Why did you take them off?

Rodney I had to give them to somebody else.

Marion rises, and slinks across to him

Marion Does that go on a lot in this place?

Rodney What?

Marion Taking off your nightclothes and giving them to other people in the middle of the afternoon.

Rodney He said they belonged to him.

Marion *He*?

Rodney Yes.

Marion And did they?

Rodney No.

Marion Then why was he so keen to have them?

Rodney I . . . I don't know.

Marion Mind you, I'm sure there are lots of people who would like to get their hands on *your* pyjama bottoms . . . (*She smiles at him, disturbingly*)

Rodney (*alarmed*) I must go! I'm looking for my clothes! (*He starts to go, stepping over the sun lounger*)

Marion Just a minute!

Rodney hesitates, nervously

You know—I could have sworn I've seen that dressing-gown somewhere before . . .

Rodney I . . . I got it from a young lady.

Marion *You* gave your pyjama bottoms to another man, and a young lady gave *you* her dressing-gown? I didn't know health farms were so sexy.

Rodney I must go!

He races out again DL

Marion laughs, enjoying the effect she has had on him and sits down to relax on the padded seat again . . .

In the bedroom . . .

Gerald comes in, carrying an armful of clothes and a travel bag. As the door opens we see there is now a number "14" on the outside. Gerald looks at the number

Gerald Ah—Fourteen . . . Right!

He comes in, happily, pushes the door shut with his foot and dumps his belongings on the bed. He looks about, approvingly

Oh, yes—this is more like it! (*He goes to look out of the window*) Aah . . . very nice.

Potter bursts in, looking very agitated

Potter Mr Corby—you can't move in here!

Gerald Yes, I can! Only too glad to get away from that car park, I can tell you. (*He chuckles, happily*)

Potter But this is Number Fourteen!

Gerald Yes, I know, and I'm very grateful. Here you are. (*He reaches for his money*) I should have thought of it before.

Potter Sorry?

Gerald holds out a five-pound note to Potter

Gerald Go on. Take it!
Rodney No, no!
Gerald Don't be daft. You deserve it. Here ... (*He takes Potter's hand and puts the note into it*)

Potter leaves his arm extended, the five-pound note sticking out of his hand like a small flag

This room is *much* better ...
Potter Yes, but you can't stay here!

Gerald immediately snatches back the five-pound note and returns it to his pocket

Gerald What do you mean I can't stay here?
Potter You've got to go back to your *own* room.
Gerald This *is* my room.
Potter No, it isn't! You've got to get out of here!
Gerald I've only just got *in* here!
Potter There's no time to argue. (*He picks up Gerald's clothes from the bed*) Come on!
Gerald Give those to me! (*He snatches them back and puts them on the bed again*)
Potter I'm trying to keep you out of trouble, sir.
Gerald What are you talking about?
Potter Your wife's downstairs!
Gerald I know that. Why didn't you bring her up?
Potter She mustn't find you in *here*! (*He picks up the clothes again*)
Gerald (*grabbing the clothes back*) Why not?
Potter (*grabbing the clothes back*) Because this is a *double* room!
Gerald (*grabbing the clothes back*) What's wrong with that? *I'm* the only person *in* it!
Potter (*quietly*) That's what *you* think ...
Gerald What?
Potter Please sir—go back to Number Six over the car park where you belong! Your wife mustn't find you in here with another woman.
Gerald Have you been drinking?
Potter (*desperately*) I wish I had, but I'm teetotal ... !
Gerald Now look here, Potter—I'm not going backwards and forwards, changing bedrooms like a bridegroom in a French farce! (*He dumps his clothes back on the bed*) I'm *here* now—in Number Fourteen—and that's where I'm staying!

He picks up his travel bag and goes out into the bathroom

(*Off*) Oh, very nice bathroom. ...

He closes the door to the bathroom, abruptly

Potter (*clasping his hands together in prayer*) "Our Father which art in Heaven, hallowed be Thy name ..."

Potter hastily picks up Gerald's clothes again and goes out, still praying, closing the door behind him

In the pool area . . .

Marion is still relaxing

Potter races in, carrying Gerald's clothes, and goes to Marion, grim-faced

Potter Bad news, I fear, Mrs Corby.

Marion I hope you're not going to embrace me again.

Potter Your husband says he's awfully sorry—he'd like to have seen you and all that—had a little chat—a cup of tea, perhaps—but he is here for treatment, you see? So he's going jogging now, then there's Mrs Maddock's massage, and after that it'll be hot soup and bed. So he sends his best wishes——

Marion Best wishes?!

Potter And he'll tell you all about it when he gets back home. (*He puts her cup and saucer down and pulls her to her feet*)

Marion You *are* going to embrace me again! Have you gone mad?

Potter (*quietly*) Not as mad as all that . . . !

Marion (*noticing the clothes he is carrying*) Where did you get those clothes from?

Potter What? (*He remembers the clothes*) Oh—these? (*Then in sudden alarm*) Ah! These! Yes . . . (*He hides them behind his back*)

Marion I've seen them somewhere before.

Potter Surely not?

Marion Let me have a look . . .

Potter No! Please! You mustn't!

Marion tries to see them. Potter dodges this way and that, and as his shoes hit the ground rhythmically, he gradually begins to execute a small Spanish dance. Marion starts to join in, clapping her hands and stamping her feet, enthusiastically, finally throwing up her arms and shouting——

Marion Olé!

Automatically, Potter follows suit

Potter Olé!

But in throwing up his arms he also throws up the clothes—high into the air! They fall all around him. He goes on to his hands and knees and gathers them up, frantically. Marion stands over him, triumphantly

Marion I thought so! What are you doing with my husband's clothes?

Potter Taking them to Oxfam.

Marion He's only had that shirt a month!

Potter He's very concerned about the Third World.

Marion I think I'll go and see what he's up to . . .

Potter (*unhappily*) Oh, no—please, madam—you mustn't do that . . .

Marion Well, I'm going to! I'll catch him before he goes jogging. Have you remembered the number of his room?

Potter (*seeing a way out*) Ah—yes! I *do* remember now! It's ... er ... it's Number Six! Overlooking the car park.

Marion Right! I'll go and find him.

As she sets off, Rodney comes back in, still without his trousers

Oh, good! I'm *so* glad you haven't found your trousers.

She smiles at him, provocatively, and goes out DL *to look for her husband*

Rodney goes to Potter

Rodney (*urgently*) Where have you put my bag?

Potter What bag?

Rodney I had a bag with me and now it's disappeared!

Potter (*vehemently*) I'm not in charge of luggage!

Rodney But my clothes are in it! I can't go about like this! (*He sees the clothes that Potter is holding*) Aah ...! (*He shoots out a finger and points at them hopefully*)

Potter No! No—you mustn't! (*He hides them behind his back*) They're not yours!

Rodney Give them to me! (*He advances on Potter*)

Potter begins to do a Spanish dance as he did before, but soon gives up

Potter (*wearily*) Oh, I can't go through all that again ...! (*He hands the clothes to Rodney*) Here!

Rodney (*surprised, but grateful*) Potter—you're a pal!

Rodney races off with the clothes through the archway UR

Potter (*disconsolately*) I've lied and I've given away another man's clothes. What is to become of me ...?

Potter goes out towards the bedrooms

The bedroom door opens on a swell of lush, romantic music (as before—"Love is a Many Splendoured Thing") which continues until the dialogue starts

We see number "14" on the outside of the door. Sandra is in the doorway. She is carrying a bottle of wine which she puts down on the armchair table. Then she gets a perfume atomizer from inside the wardrobe cupboard, sprays herself and the general atmosphere, liberally, replaces the atomizer and goes to draw the curtains

The room darkens a little. She turns on the bedside light, and is pleased with the effect. Then she lies down on the bed, decoratively, smiling in wicked anticipation

Gerald comes out of the bathroom. He is wearing brightly coloured boxer shorts and a blue vest, and is carrying his dressing-gown which he puts down on the armchair. Then he turns and sees Sandra and reacts in alarm. The music stops

Gerald Sandra! (*He pulls in his stomach with masculine pride*) What are *you* doing in here?

Sandra Waiting for you.
Gerald You can't lie down there!
Sandra Nobody can see us. I've drawn the curtains.

Gerald glances, briefly, at the curtains

Gerald (*aggrieved*) I can't see the view now ...
Sandra There's a better one over here ...
Gerald (*clapping his hands, imperiously*) Come on! Off you go—back to your own room!
Sandra This *is* my room.
Gerald No, it isn't. It's *my* room!
Sandra Whatever gave you that idea?
Gerald I've been moved! Don't you remember? Into Number Fourteen.
Sandra But Number Fourteen is *my* room.
Gerald Now look, Sandra—I enjoy a joke as much as the next man, and we've had a good laugh, the two of us, haven't we? (*He laughs, briefly, then claps his hands again*) But now up you get and off you go! (*He pulls her off the bed*)
Sandra (*smiling and going towards the bathroom*) Have you hung up your clothes yet? (*She goes out into the bathroom*)
Gerald (*calling*) I haven't had time, have I?

Sandra returns with two plastic glasses and puts them down with the wine

Sandra (*innocently*) Why don't you look in the wardrobe?
Gerald What?
Sandra Make sure there's *room* for *your* clothes. ...

Gerald stares at her, frozen, for a moment, then races across to the wardrobe cupboard, opens it, looks inside, slams it shut again and leans against it, looking at her, appalled

Gerald It's *your* room!
Sandra That's what I told you ...
Gerald (*like a man awaiting the gallows*) What am I doing in your room?
Sandra That's what a lot of people will want to know ... (*She goes to him, seductively*) But *I* won't tell them if *you* don't ...
Gerald You said Mr Potter had found me a better room.
Sandra (*smiling*) Yes. ... I know ...
Gerald (*appalled*) You made it up!!
Sandra Yes ... I know ... Aren't you pleased?
Gerald No, I'm not! This is a health farm. I'm supposed to go back home feeling better for it!
Sandra You *will* ... !

A knock at the door. Gerald reacts in alarm

Gerald Oh, my God ... ! (*He whispers to her, urgently*) You'll have to get out of here!
Sandra It'll only be Mr Potter.
Marion (*off*) Gerry, darling!

Gerald That's not Mr Potter . . . !
Sandra Sounds like somebody who knows you.
Gerald It is! Come on—quickly! (*He hustles her towards the bathroom*)
Sandra Where are we going?
Gerald *You're* going into the bathroom. (*He opens the bathroom door*)
Sandra (*giggling, happily*) Oo, hide and seek! What fun!

Gerald does not think it is fun and pushes her, abruptly, into the bathroom and closes the door after her

> *He hastens across and opens the door to the corridor. Marion is there. She looks at his attire in surprise*

Marion Oh, Gerry—you do look sexy!

Gerald looks down, sees his coloured shorts and vest, and hastily grabs his dressing-gown and puts it on

Marion closes the door and looks about

> It's very dark in here. Are you having a séance?

Gerald races to the window and draws back the curtains, abruptly, then to the bedside table to switch off the lamp

> You took a long time opening the door.

Gerald I was lying down. (*He lies on the bed*)
Marion In the middle of the afternoon?
Gerald It's part of the treatment.
Marion I thought you were going jogging?
Gerald Was I?
Marion Good heavens! It smells like a lady's boudoir in here. Don't tell me you've changed your after-shave?
Gerald It's the air freshener! It's the same in all the rooms.
Marion How very sexy. No wonder you all go to bed in the afternoon. (*She lies down next to him*) I thought you were in Number Six?

He escapes, hastily

Gerald I was. But I've been moved. So how did you know where to find me?
Marion I spoke to a large man on the landing. He said he saw you disappearing in here with a bundle of clothes and a smile on your face.
Gerald What are you doing in here, anyway? I left you at home. (*He glances, nervously, towards the bathroom*)
Marion Well, I was on my way to visit somebody and realized it was quite near here, so I thought I'd pop in and see what it's like. I've never been to a health farm before.
Gerald You won't like it! (*He pulls her off the bed and propels her towards the door*) Go and have a word with Linda!
Marion Linda?
Gerald Yes.
Marion (*puzzled*) *Our* Linda?
Gerald Yes!

Marion Is she on the telephone?
Gerald No, no! She's staying here!
Marion I didn't know that. You must have been very surprised to see her.
Gerald I was . . . !
Marion And then *I* turned up! Quite a family reunion. We ought to be on
This Is Your Life. (*She goes towards the bathroom*) Is it through here?
Gerald What?!
Marion The bathroom.
Gerald No!
Marion What?

He races across to intercept her

Gerald You can't go in there!
Marion Gerry, I've had a long journey and I want to go to the bathroom.
Gerald You can't!
Marion I must!

She pushes him aside and continues towards the bathroom

A knock at the door

Gerald (*quietly*) Saved by the knock . . .
Marion What a busy bedroom.

Gerald opens the door. Potter comes in

Potter Good heavens! It smells like a lady's boudoir in here!
Marion When were *you* last in a lady's boudoir?
Potter (*seeing Marion and going to her, distressed*) Oh, dear. You found
him, Mrs Corby . . .
Marion *You* told me he was in Number Six.
Potter I wish he *was* . . .
Gerald So do I . . .
Marion Why? This is a very nice room.
Potter But he doesn't like it. Do you, sir?
Gerald No. I don't like it at all.
Potter He prefers Number Six.
Marion Over the car park?
Gerald Yes. I miss the smell of petrol.
Potter So we're going to move him back in there.
Marion Gerry, you can't keep moving from place to place like a gypsy. This
is a lovely room. You should be pleased.
Gerald Yes. I know. I thought I would be. But I'm not.
Marion Such a big bed.
Gerald Far *too* big.
Marion You like a big bed to stretch in. And you'll have plenty of room in
this one.
Potter (*quietly*) I wouldn't be too sure about that . . . !
Gerald It's north facing!
Marion What?

Gerald The bed. I'll have dreams if I face north.
Potter You certainly will . . . !
Gerald That's settled, then! Off we go! Back to Number Six!

Gerald and Potter start to go

Marion Good heavens! There's a bottle of wine over here!

Gerald and Potter stop

Gerald What?
Potter (*aghast*) Wine? We don't allow alcohol on the premises!
Marion Well, there's some over here.

Potter looks at Gerald, deeply disillusioned

Potter Oh, Mr Corby . . . the pillars of morality appear to be trembling
    again . . .
Gerald It's not mine!
Marion And two glasses . . . ! Were you expecting a guest?
Gerald No! No!
Marion Two noes?
Gerald One for each glass.
Marion Then why is there a bottle of red wine in your bedroom?

Gerald has a sudden inspiration and goes to her, urgently

Gerald Ah—yes—of course—I forgot!
Marion Forgot what?
Gerald That's not red wine.
Marion Looks like red wine to me.
Potter (*the voice of doom*) And to *me* . . . !
Gerald You can't always go by outside appearances.
Marion You mean it's a bottle of milk in disguise?
Gerald (*forcing a laugh*) Oh, darling! You are funny! A bottle of—(*turning
    to Potter*) Isn't she funny?

He sees Potter's grim face

    No, never mind . . .
Marion But if it isn't red wine, Gerry—what *is* it?
Potter (*severely*) Yes, Mr Corby—what *is* it?
Gerald Well, it's . . . it's—it's medicinal!
Potter Medicinal?
Gerald Yes. Good for the blood. That's why it's red. Made by monks.
    Often used in health farms. It's a . . . a sort of . . . syrup. A cordial. Full of
    iron. Very good for the nerves.
Potter (*quietly*) It'll need to be . . . !
Gerald And that's it really—(*recapitulating, briefly*)—red liquid, good for
    health, made by monks, sort of cordial.
Potter So what do you think, Mrs Corby? True or bluff?

Gerald glares at Potter

Marion But what exactly are the ingredients, Gerry?

Gerald Ah—well—nobody knows, do they?

Marion Why don't you ask the monks?

Gerald It's a silent order.

Marion (*considering carefully*) But if what you say is true ... why does the label on the bottle say Beaujolais?

Gerald (*in huge astonishment*) Beaujolais? (*He goes to inspect the bottle and then turns to glare at Potter*) Potter! How the hell did *this* get in here?

Potter *I* don't know!

Gerald Well, *think* of something!

Potter wilts under Gerald's threatening gaze

Potter I ... I suppose there must be a ... a secret drinker on the staff ... (*He lowers his head in shame, having uttered another lie*)

Gerald smiles broadly, takes Potter's face in his hands and kisses him on the forehead

Gerald Of course! Why didn't *I* think of that? (*To Marion*) Did you hear that, darling? A secret drinker. (*He kisses her on the forehead also*) Well, well! Now we know, eh? (*He laughs, relieved*)

Marion That doesn't explain why there's a bottle of wine in your bedroom.

Gerald Doesn't it? Oh. (*He turns to Potter again*) Got anything else, Potter?

Potter (*defiantly*) No ... !

Gerald Yes, you have!

Reluctantly, Potter proceeds to put another nail in his moral coffin

Potter Well ... presumably the secret drinker ... had ...

Gerald (*helpfully*) Too much to drink?

Potter Very possibly.

Gerald And?

Potter And ... and left red wine in here ... in mistake for the monks' medicinal cordial ...

Gerald takes Potter's face in his hands and kisses him on the forehead again

Gerald There! That wasn't very difficult, was it? (*To Marion*) There you are, you see? I knew there was a simple explanation. (*He kisses her also*)

At that moment the lavatory flushes in the bathroom noisily. They all freeze, astonished at this

Marion Gerry ... ?

Gerald Yes?

Marion I think there's somebody in your bathroom.

Gerald Don't be silly. How could anybody get in there?

Marion Then your lavatory must have an automatic flush. (*She goes towards the bathroom*)

Gerald looks at Potter, who shakes his head, mournfully

Potter Oh, no, sir—she *isn't* ... ?

Gerald (*nodding in despair*) Oh, yes, sir—she *is* ...!

Marion opens the bathroom door

Marion Perhaps you'd like to come in and join the party?

Sandra comes in from the bathroom, nervously

Sandra Hallo ...
Gerald (*glaring at her*) Why did you have to go and use the lavatory?
Sandra Well, I've been in there so long ...
Marion Gerry—aren't you going to introduce us?
Gerald Ah—yes. This is Marion.
Marion I know who *I* am. I want to know who *she* is.
Sandra Who's Marion?
Marion I'm Gerry's wife.
Sandra Wife?!
Marion Don't you know what a wife is?
Sandra Yes, but I didn't think he'd got one with him.
Marion Well, he has—and it's me! Who the hell are *you*, and why are you hiding in my husband's bathroom?
Gerald She wasn't hiding!
Potter The moral fabric of this establishment has suddenly become thread-bare ... (*He sinks on to the bed in despair*)
Marion If she wasn't hiding what was she doing in there?
Gerald Cleaning!
Marion }
Sandra } (*together*) Cleaning?!
Gerald Yes! She's on the staff here. Isn't she, Potter?
Potter Don't speak to me. I'm too depressed ...
Marion (*to Sandra*) And that's why you were in the bathroom?
Sandra Yes. (*Demurely*) I'm a chambermaid.
Potter (*looking up*) Chamber*person*! We can't have any sex in here!
Marion (*smiling like a razor*) Of *course* you're a chambermaid! I should have guessed. You're wearing the new summer uniform.
Gerald (*abruptly, anxious to be rid of her*) You've finished your cleaning now, haven't you, Sandra? (*He grabs her and pushes her towards the door*)
Marion Sandra? Is that her name?
Gerald Yes. Isn't it?
Marion I didn't think you'd know.
Gerald She was wearing a badge when I arrived. It said "Sandra". Right across here. (*He indicates Sandra's chest*)
Marion And you noticed it, of course.
Gerald I couldn't miss it.
Marion No. I'm *sure* you couldn't. ...
Gerald (*to Sandra*) If you've finished you can *go*! I'm sure you've got plenty to do ... *elsewhere*!
Sandra Yes, Mr Corby. (*She smiles, nervously, at Marion*) Nice to meet you, Mrs Corby.

She is about to go, then remembers something. She goes and picks up the bottle of wine

I may as well take this with me, then.

She walks out with the bottle of wine

Marion looks after her, astonished. Gerald puts his arm around Potter, proudly

Gerald You see? Mr Potter was right. There *was* a secret drinker on the staff.
Marion Yes. Wasn't that lucky?
Gerald What?

Gerald hastily picks up the plastic glasses, takes them back into the bathroom

Marion (*as he returns*) Gerry—is it all right if I use the bathroom now? Or have you got any *more* young ladies hidden away?
Gerald Oh, darling! You are funny! Young ladies—(*turning to Potter*) Isn't she funny?

He sees Potter's grim face

No—never mind. (*To Marion*) You carry on, darling. There's nobody else in there.
Marion There'd better not be. . . .

She goes into the bathroom, closing the door after her

Gerald turns to Potter, delightedly

Gerald Well done, Potter! (*He kisses him on the forehead*)
Potter (*piously*) I'm a moral man and I disapprove of lies . . .
Gerald You're a genius!
Potter (*rising in despair*) I'm a liar! I shall never raise my head in decent society again.
Gerald Of course you will. Look—you'd better go and have a word with her.
Potter Who?
Gerald Sandra! Tell her to keep out of sight.
Potter Why?

Gerald casts a quick, anxious glance towards the bathroom

Gerald Because we can't have my wife seeing Sandra sitting by the swimming-pool when she's supposed to be on the staff! So go and keep her out of the way!

He pushes Potter, unceremoniously, out of the door and closes it, abruptly, after him as Marion returns from the bathroom

Marion I can't think why you don't like this room, Gerry. It's delightful.

Gerald It's too big. I have a fear of open spaces. So I'm going back to my little room over the car park.

Gerald goes out into the bathroom

Marion (*calling*) Oh, all right, then. Please yourself. I'll go and say hallo to Linda.

Gerald returns with his travel bag

Gerald I thought you were in a hurry to get to your friend?
Marion Darling, I can't go without seeing Linda, now can I?
Gerald Oh, all right. But don't take all day about it! (*He opens the door to the corridor*)
Marion She's got *such* a pretty face ...

Gerald hesitates in the doorway

Gerald Who?
Marion The secret drinking chamberperson.
Gerald (*deliberately vague*) Really? I hadn't noticed.

He goes, quickly. Marion smiles, suspiciously, and goes out after him, closing the door behind her

In the pool area ...

Linda comes in from UR. She is now wearing a bathing costume and carrying a towel. At the same time Sandra comes in from the bedrooms, carrying the bottle of wine. They are both looking gloomy. They stop when they see each other

Sandra *You* don't look very happy ...
Linda Neither do you ...
Sandra His wife's turned up. (*She sits on the sun lounger, miserably*)
Linda Your boss's wife?
Sandra Yes.
Linda Oh, dear. (*She sits beside her*)
Sandra How about *your* chap?
Linda He's gone.
Sandra Gone?
Linda He was frightened my father might catch him.
Sandra You mean your *father's* staying here, too?
Linda Yes.
Sandra Well, that's that, then, isn't it?
Linda Yes ...
Sandra What are we going to do?
Linda I suppose we'll just have to concentrate on the treatment ...
Sandra Saunas and swimming and no ... ?
Linda Yes ...

They contemplate the thought without enthusiasm

Potter comes racing in, grabs the astonished Sandra by the arm and starts to drag her away towards the archway UR

Potter Come on! Off we go! You can't hang about here!

Sandra Why not?

Potter (*distractedly*) Because you mustn't be seen sitting by the swimming-pool as if you were a guest!

Linda She *is* a guest!

Potter (*long-suffering*) Yes. *You* know that, and *she* knows that, and *I* know that—but some people *don't* know that! (*He grabs the wine from Sandra and hands it to Linda, abruptly*) Take that away and hide it! It mustn't be seen here!

Linda (*bewildered*) But surely——?

Potter Do as I say!

Linda Oh—very well . . .

She goes out towards the bedrooms with the bottle of wine

Potter *You* mustn't be seen here, either, so come on! Off we go!

He drags the surprised Sandra out through the archway UR

In the bedroom . . .

The door opens and Linda comes in. We see that number "10" is on the door again. She looks at the wine, shrugs, puts it down on the armchair table and goes into the bathroom to change

Rodney appears outside the window on the same flood of romantic music that heralded Sandra's arrival before. He peers in to make sure the coast is clear, and then climbs into the room. He is now wearing Gerald's clothes (which are too small or too big for him). He is carrying a plastic shopping bag. He goes to make sure that the door to the corridor is locked

Linda returns, finishing putting on a sundress, sees him and looks delighted

The music fades

Linda Rodney!

Rodney (*jumping a mile*) Aaaah!

Linda You've come back!

Rodney I had to.

Linda I hoped you would . . .

Rodney I couldn't find my clothes.

Linda I *thought* those weren't the ones you arrived in . . . (*She peers at his clothes and giggles*) Where did you get them from?

Rodney tries to appear normal in his ill-fitting clothes

Rodney I . . . I borrowed them.

Linda Couldn't you have borrowed something more your size? (*She cannot control her laughter*)

Rodney stands there, feeling ridiculous, trying to remain dignified in the face of her amusement

Rodney Have you quite finished?

Linda I'm sorry, Rodney . . . (*She tries to pull herself together*) It's just that . . . that you don't look very sexy dressed like that. (*She laughs again*)

Rodney (*fed up*) Right! That's it, then! I'll go home like this!

Linda No, no—don't go! (*She wipes the tears of laughter from her eyes*) I promise I won't laugh any more. (*She assumes a more sober mien and smiles at him, warmly*) I'm glad you came back ...

Rodney (*sheepishly*) Good ...

Linda And I've got something nice for you.

Rodney Yes—I know you have. ...

Linda You'll never guess what it is.

Rodney (*grinning*) I bet I will ... !

Linda runs across to pick up the bottle of wine. She holds it out to show him

Linda There!

He stares at the bottle in surprise

Rodney Red wine? I thought you weren't allowed alcohol in this place?

Linda You aren't, but *I* won't tell if *you* don't!

Rodney All right, then—now I'll show you what *I*'ve got for *you* ...

Linda (*pretending to be shocked*) Not *now*, Rodney!

Rodney No, no—not that! (*He holds up the plastic bag*) Supper!

Linda (*moved*) Oh, Rodney—you've brought me a food parcel ...

Rodney Go on, then—look inside!

He holds the bag open under her nose. Linda peers inside. Then she looks up at him, incredulously

Linda It's *not*!

Rodney It is!

Linda Chinese food?

Rodney Yes!

Linda Where did you get it?

Rodney There's a take-away in the village.

Linda But you can't bring that in here!

Rodney Why not?

Linda This is a health farm! You're not allowed stuff like that.

Rodney *I* won't tell anyone if *you* don't!

They laugh, happily

We'll start starving tomorrow. (*He hands her the bag*) You sort out the food, and I'll open the wine. (*He stops*) Oh, my God!

Linda What?

Rodney We haven't got an opener!

Linda is taking the silver foil containers out of the carrier bag on the armchair table

Linda Didn't you bring one?

Rodney Why should I bring one? I thought we'd be staying in an hotel.

Linda What are we going to do, then?

Rodney Ring reception. They'll send one up.

Linda And let them know we're drinking wine?

Rodney If we don't we *won't* be.

Linda We can't!

Rodney (*wearily*) All right. Here I go again. I'll have to go and get one. (*He starts to get out of the window*)

Linda (*following*) Where from?

Rodney The Chinese take-away. They're very co-operative. I bet they get lots of starving people from here creeping out for sustenance. Shan't be long! (*He starts to disappear down the ladder*)

Linda (*calling after him*) And bring some chopsticks!

Rodney (*off*) Righto ... !

He has gone

Linda smiles, happily, and goes back to sorting out the containers. The aroma is obviously delicious

There is a knock at the door. Linda freezes in alarm

Linda Oh, my God ... ! (*Calling*) Who is it?

Marion (*off*) It's me, darling!

Linda Who?

Marion (*off*) Me—your dear old mother!

Linda looks appalled

Linda Oh, no ... ! (*Calling*) Just a minute!

She races back to the window and leans out to call Rodney

Rodney! (*But it is too late*) Oh, hell ... !

Another knock at the door

Marion (*off*) Come on! Let me in!

Linda (*calling*) Just coming!

She races across to the door, then remembers the Chinese food. She hastens back, quickly puts the containers back into the bag, dithers with it uncertainly, and then shoves it under the bed. She goes and opens the door to reveal Marion

Marion Surprise! Surprise!

Linda It certainly is ... !

Marion comes in, and they embrace. Linda shuts the door

Why aren't you at home?

Marion I'm going to visit Mr Johnson.

Linda (*blankly*) Who?

Marion Our old gardener! Surely you remember? He was with us for years. He was very particular about his petunias.

Linda (*distracted*) Oh—yes—of course!

Marion Well, he's over eighty now and he *so* loves a visit.

Linda But Mr Johnson doesn't live *here*!

Marion No, but he lives nearby. So I thought I'd pop in and see your father on the way. But what on earth are *you* doing here?

Linda I . . . I thought it would make a change.

Marion What a lovely room! It's *just* like the one your father's in. Have you got a nice view? (*She goes to look*) Good heavens!

Linda (*fearful*) What is it?

Marion He's left his ladder outside your window!

Linda A ladder?! (*She hastens to the window, over-doing her surprise*) How on earth did that get there?

Marion It belongs to the window-cleaner. You'd better have it removed.

Linda No!

Marion What?

Linda He . . . he might need it.

Marion You can't leave a ladder outside your bedroom window all night. Somebody might get in. I'll ask reception to take it away. (*She heads for the telephone*)

Linda No! *I'll* do it!

Marion stops, looking puzzled

Marion Darling . . . ?

Linda Yes?

Marion You'll probably think I'm being awfully silly, but—(*sniffing the air a little*)—I can smell cooking.

Linda (*alarmed*) What?!

They both freeze

Black-out bedroom lighting

In the pool area . . .

> *Gerald comes in from the bedrooms, urgently, carrying his bag. At the same time Potter comes in* UR, *looking forlorn. They meet and collide*

Gerald } (*together*) Aaaah!
Potter

Potter (*fearfully*) Oh, Mr Corby—are you going where I think you're going?

Gerald I'm going to get the key!

Potter What key?

Gerald The key to Number Six, of course!

Potter Your old room over the car park?

Gerald Yes, of course! That's where I'm going, isn't it?

Potter You can't!

Gerald I must! I'm not sharing a room with my secretary! You should be pleased, Potter. I thought you *wanted* me to go back to the car park.

Potter Yes. I did. But now it's too late.

Gerald Too late?

Potter Did you tell Miss Figgis at reception that you were moving into Number Fourteen?

Gerald Yes, but I didn't know it was Sandra's room then!

Potter Well, now Miss Figgis has let your room to someone else!

Gerald Who?

Potter The plumber.

Gerald (*pleased*) Ah! You've found a plumber at last?

Potter Yes. And he's in your room.

Gerald He's supposed to be mending the steam bath not going to bed!

Potter He was so tired. Poor man. Miss Figgis took pity on him. He'd come fifty miles. On his bicycle!

Gerald That's a long way to go for a plumber.

Potter He was the only one we could get. And *he* only came when Miss Figgis promised him a room for the night.

Gerald *My* room!

Potter Yes. He's in there now. Unpacking his tools.

Gerald So either I share a double room with Sandra or a single room with the plumber?

Potter (*thinking hard*) There must be another alternative . . .

Gerald There *is*! I'm going to get the plumber out of Number Six! (*He starts to go*)

Potter No! You can't do that! He'll refuse to see to the pipes!

Gerald marches out, briskly, towards the bedrooms, pursued by a protesting Potter

Lights up in the bedroom

Marion There's definitely a smell of cooking. (*She goes about the room sniffing like a tracker dog*)

Linda It'll be the fumes from the cooking in the kitchen!

Marion Don't be silly. You live on raw vegetables here. They don't *have* to cook.

Linda Soup!!

Marion What?

Linda They cook soup. That's what you can smell. Chicken soup! (*She mimes a chicken flapping its wings*) Coming through the window!

Marion I don't think it *is* coming through the window . . . (*She goes to check*)

Linda instantly grabs her mother by the arm and swings her round, recklessly, diverting her in the direction of the door

Marion, naturally, is somewhat surprised

Linda It was lovely to see you, Mummy—such a nice surprise—but don't let me hold you up any longer! Mr Johnson will be wondering where you are—so—(*she kisses her mother twice, very briefly, in rapid succession*)— goodbye, Mother!

Marion You're very keen to get rid of me.

Linda You hate driving in the dark.

Marion I know I drive slowly, but I think even *I* can manage ten miles before nightfall. (*She escapes from Linda towards the armchair table*)

Linda looks desperate

Marion sees the red wine

Oh, good!

Linda (*nervously*) What?

Marion I see *you've* got some of the monks' medicinal cordial! (*She picks up the bottle*)

Linda I thought it was red wine.

Marion What? (*She looks more closely at the label and goes to Linda*) Good heavens! *This* one's Beaujolais, as well! This shouldn't be in here!

Linda I know ... !

Marion (*confidentially*) There's a secret drinker amongst the staff, you know ...

And at that moment, Rodney arrives at the top of the ladder, leans in through the window with a big smile and announces, proudly——

Rodney There we are! Chopsticks and a bottle opener!

Linda freezes in horror. Marion gazes at Rodney, who is holding out the items referred to. She has raised the bottle of wine like a club. Hold the picture

Linda suddenly grabs her mother around the waist and clings on to her, dramatically, seeking protection

Linda Oh, *Mummy!* There's a burglar!

Rodney (*appalled*) M-m-mummy ... ?

Marion If he was a burglar he'd hardly arrive carrying chopsticks and a bottle opener.

Marion realizes that she is still holding the bottle of wine and hastily hands it to Linda, who puts it down on the bedside table. Marion goes to Rodney

I see you're back at the top of the ladder. I wondered where you'd got to.

Linda You *know* this burglar?

Marion We have met, yes, and he's not a burglar. (*She smiles, encouragingly, at Rodney*) Do come in and join the party ...

Rodney I ... I think I've come into the wrong room. I was looking for number——

Marion Come on in.

Rodney Well, that's very kind of you—but I'd better be going ... (*He starts to go down the ladder*)

Marion (*loudly*) Come on in!

Rodney climbs in through the window, obediently. Marion circles him slowly, looking in surprise at his ill-fitting clothes. Rodney shifts, self-consciously, under her gaze, the chopsticks and bottle opener now behind his back

You know, I've only ever seen you on two occasions. And both times you've been wearing clothes that I'm sure I've seen somewhere before ... (*She sits in the armchair, gazing at him intently*)

Linda goes, quickly, to her mother

Linda Mummy! If you don't go soon it'll be dark!

Marion It may be an old car but it does have headlights.
Linda But you don't like driving in the dark! You really must go!
Marion And leave you with this intruder?
Linda He's trying to go! He *wants* to go!
Rodney Yes! I'm in the wrong room!
Marion Well, you *can't* go!
Linda Why not?
Marion Because *I* want to know why he's carrying chopsticks and a bottle opener. (*To Rodney*) So come on! I'm not moving from here until I get an explanation.

Rodney and Linda exchange an anguished look. He realizes that he will have to think of an explanation and reluctantly starts to extemporize . . .

Rodney Oh. Er . . . well, you see . . . I—I'd been out jogging.
Marion Dressed like that?
Rodney Ah—no. I . . . I was wearing shorts then.
Marion (*smiling*) I wish I'd seen you. . . .
Rodney I was running quite quickly, as a matter of fact. About five miles an hour, I should think. Around the garden.
Marion *This* garden?
Rodney Yes. And as I approached the gates, I noticed . . . two men . . . coming in.
Marion Coming in here?
Rodney Yes. Arriving. You know. On foot. And we . . . we got into conversation.
Marion While you were still running?
Rodney Ah—no. I stopped running when they started talking.
Marion What were they talking *about*?
Rodney Well . . . they said . . . that they were going to spend some time here.
Marion At the health farm?
Rodney Yes. And I said, "I didn't know that Chinese people went to health farms".

Marion considers this

Marion You didn't say that they were Chinese.
Rodney Didn't I? Well, they were. Both of them. I could tell straight away. Anyhow, we got talking—you know how one does——
Marion In Chinese?
Rodney Sorry?
Marion Was your conversation conducted in Chinese?
Rodney Oh, no. No. They spoke very good English. A bit of an accent, but nothing I couldn't cope with. And they said it was going to be very hard doing without food here. And I said, "Yes, I imagine you will feel the difference. Especially being Chinese. You'll keep feeling hungry again". And they said—and you're going to find this very difficult to believe— they said, "As we won't be eating very much for a week or so, would you be very kind and look after these until we get out?" (*And he holds up the chopsticks, triumphantly*)

Marion and Linda are speechless

The door bursts open, and Gerald and Potter come in, Gerald still carrying his travel bag

Rodney hastily hides the chopsticks and bottle opener. Gerald and Potter are surprised to see Rodney there

Gerald Oh, no! Not *you* again!
Marion He came in through the window.
Gerald He always does.
Marion Have you seen him before, then?
Gerald Oh, yes. We had quite a chat. *You're* taking a long time to say goodbye to Linda.
Marion Something unexpected cropped up.
Linda (*quietly*) It certainly did . . . !
Marion Anyway, what are *you* doing here? I thought you were moving back to the car park.
Gerald That damn plumber refuses to leave. He's barricaded himself in!
Marion (*bewildered*) What *are* you talking about . . . ?

Gerald looks more closely at Rodney's ill-fitting clothes

Gerald Have you been in the swimming-pool with your clothes on?
Rodney No! (*He tries to make his clothes appear more adequate*)
Gerald Well, they don't seem to fit very well!
Rodney They're not mine . . .
Potter (*hastily*) He borrowed them! Didn't you, sir?
Rodney No, I didn't! You gave them to me!
Gerald I'm sure I've seen them somewhere before . . . (*He peers at them*)
Potter No! No, you haven't! You've never seen them before in your life!
Gerald I've got a shirt just like that. . . .
Potter No, you haven't!
Marion I thought I recognized it. He's wearing my husband's clothes! The ones you said you were taking to Oxfam, Mr Potter.

Gerald looks apalled and turns to glare at Potter, who cringes, apprehensively

Gerald You were taking my clothes to *Oxfam*?!
Potter No! To the cleaners!
Gerald So why did you give them to him?
Potter He was running about without any trousers.
Marion (*smiling at the pleasant memory*) Yes—I *saw* him . . .
Gerald What happened to your *own* clothes?
Rodney I lost them. My suitcase has disappeared. You don't want me to take them off *now*, do you?

Potter leaps in front of Rodney, arms outstretched, trying to hide him from the ladies

Potter No! Not in front of the ladies!
Marion (*quietly*) Oh, what a pity . . . !

Gerald (*to Rodney, as if to a child*) You keep coming into the wrong room. Have you got no sense of direction? Your room's further along.
Rodney I never was good at geography.
Gerald Your girl-friend must be wondering what's happened to you.
Rodney Sorry?
Gerald She'll be waiting for you to "storm the battlements". . . .
Rodney (*remembering*) Ah—yes! I suppose she will . . .
Gerald She'll be going off the boil if you don't catch her soon! (*He laughs*)
Marion What are you talking about, Gerry?
Gerald He's been having trouble with his girl-friend.
Potter Yes, he has . . . !
Gerald So I gave him a bit of advice.
Marion As an expert?
Gerald As an exp——No! I thought you were leaving?
Linda Yes, Mummy—I'll come and see you out! (*She takes Marion towards the door*)
Marion Everybody wants to get rid of me . . .
Linda We're only thinking about your driving.
Gerald Her driving doesn't *bear* thinking about . . . Anyway, won't your old friend be expecting you?
Marion Oh—yes! I mustn't be late. (*She kisses Gerald, briefly*) Goodbye, then, Gerry. I'll leave you to it.
Gerald What? Oh—yes. Right. Goodbye, darling.

Marion smiles, provocatively, at Rodney

Marion I do hope you go through the *right* window next time.

Marion goes out with Linda

Gerald (*to Rodney*) Off you go, then! Don't keep her waiting any longer! (*He urges him out of the window*)
Potter (*suddenly*) Mr Corby!
Gerald What is it, Potter?

Potter is standing still, concentrating hard, his eyes moving from left to right, his nostrils twitching as he sniffs the air like a rabbit. He moves about slowly, sniffing all the time, gradually going lower and lower as he follows the scent

Gerald and Rodney watch him: Gerald in surprise, Rodney in fear (one leg out of the window)

Potter goes down on to his hands and knees and crawls around the bed, sniffing lower and lower, his face almost touching the carpet. Then he reaches under the bed with one outstretched hand. Gerald goes to him, intrigued

What *are* you looking for . . . ?
Potter Well, whatever it is, sir, I've found it!

He produces the plastic shopping bag containing Chinese food. He and Gerald look astonished. Rodney is frozen with fear

Potter opens the top of the bag carefully and peers inside, as if fearful that it might be a bomb. He sniffs again and looks up at Gerald, perplexed

Chinese food!!

Rodney slips and falls, spectacularly, off the ladder, disappearing from sight outside, calling as he goes

Rodney A-a-a-a-a-a-ah ... !

Potter and Gerald look at each other in alarm

Gerald races out, carrying his bag

Potter starts to follow with the Chinese food, then notices the bottle of wine on the bedside table. In appalled disapproval, he quickly grabs the bottle of wine

Potter hastens out after Gerald, closing the door behind him

In the pool area ...

Marion and Linda come in from the bedrooms, talking

Marion Goodbye, then, darling. I do hope you can settle down and enjoy the rest of your stay. (*She kisses her, briefly*)
Linda So do I ... !

Gerald comes running in from the bedrooms, still carrying his bag and muttering despairingly

Gerald Oh dear, oh dear, oh dear, oh dear ... ! (*He disappears through the archway* UR)

Potter races in. He hesitates between the ladies and holds up the bottle of wine, disapprovingly

Potter Oh dear, oh dear, oh dear, oh dear ... ! (*He runs out after Gerald*)
Marion I wonder what *they're* up to ... ? You know, Gerry's been behaving very strangely since I arrived.

Sandra comes in from the pool. She is now in another bright bathing suit and is carrying a towel

She does not see Linda and Marion, and settles down on her towel to relax. Marion sees her and whispers urgently to Linda

There she is!
Linda Who?
Marion The secret drinker!
Linda Don't be silly, Mother. That's Sandra.
Marion You know her?
Linda Of course!
Marion I'm surprised the staff are allowed to use the facilities ...
Linda (*laughing*) Sandra's not one of the staff!
Marion Of course she is!
Linda No, Mummy! (*Calling*) Hallo, Sandra!

Sandra turns and sees them. She races across to them, subserviently

Sandra I'm so sorry, madam. I didn't think anyone was here, so I thought I'd have a swim while nobody was looking. I do apologize. It won't happen again. Please don't tell the manager. Can I get you anything, madam?

Marion (*graciously*) No, thank you, dear.

Sandra Very well, madam. If you'll excuse me——

Linda (*bewildered*) Sandra! Come and sit down ...

Sandra That's very kind of you, miss. But we're not allowed to mix with the guests.

And she darts out into the steam bath (which is not where she meant to go) and shuts the door behind her

Marion She's right, Linda. You mustn't keep her from her work.

Linda She doesn't work here! She's a guest. Staying here all on her own. Well, she was until her boss arrived.

Marion Her boss?

Linda Yes. She's his secretary. He's quite a bit older than she is, apparently, but she says he rather fancies her. So she was hoping that they might ... you know. (*She giggles*)

Marion "You know"?

Linda Yes.

Marion But they haven't?

Linda I don't think so.

Marion Why not?

Linda His wife's turned up unexpectedly!

Marion Good heavens ... !

They both laugh at the thought. Then they react and turn to look at each other as their laughter dies

Marion Are you thinking what *I'm* thinking?

She is, but——

Linda No!

Marion Well, *I* am! (*She sits down on the sun lounger, decisively*)

Linda I thought you were going?

Marion I've changed my mind.

Sandra bursts out of the steam bath, breathing heavily

Sandra I didn't mean to go in there ... (*She sees them still there and staggers across to them*) Can I get you a tray of tea, madam? Buttered toast? Chocolate cake? Scones and——?

Marion You needn't bother with all that. You're Mr Corby's secretary, aren't you?

Sandra looks at Linda, who shrugs helplessly, then looks back at Marion

Sandra Yes ...

Marion Well—fancy you both being here at the same time ... How cosy!

Sandra (*defensively*) Nothing happened!

Marion Then what were you doing in his bedroom?
Sandra It's not his bedroom! It's mine!
Marion Ah! So he was in *your* room! *And* wearing sexy shorts. (*She gets up, abruptly*)
Linda (*hopefully*) Are you going?

Marion smiles, relishing the prospect

Marion Yes. I'm going to give him a nice surprise!

Marion walks out, briskly, towards the bedrooms

Linda looks at Sandra, guiltily

Linda Sorry. I didn't realize that your boss was my father. . . .
Sandra Your *father*?! Oh, no . . . !

They start to laugh and sit on the sun lounger as . . .

Gerald comes striding in from the archway

He stops, seeing them laughing together. He tries to join in their laughter, but soon fails

Gerald Er . . . have you two met, then?
Linda 'Course we have, Daddy.
Sandra 'Course we have, Daddy.
Gerald Ah . . .
Linda Why didn't you tell me that your secretary was here? Did you bring her along to take notes?

The girls giggle, which infuriates Gerald

Gerald I didn't bring her! Did I, Sandra?
Sandra (*deliberately vague*) Didn't you, Mr Corby?
Gerald You know very well I didn't! We met here by accident!
Linda Doesn't seem likely . . .
Sandra No . . .
Linda Bit of a coincidence . . .
Sandra Yes . . .
Gerald Sandra—you know very well what happened!
Linda Oh? Something did happen, then?
Gerald No! Nothing! That's what happened! Nothing!
Sandra There's still time . . .
Linda Anyway, it doesn't really matter, does it?
Gerald Doesn't it?
Linda No. It's what people will *think* happened that matters . . .

Gerald looks far from reassured

Potter comes in, anxiously, from the archway

Potter You're taking a long time finding a blanket, Mr Corby. I've got a man lying on his back out there!
Sandra (*giggling*) I wish *I* had . . . !

Linda Why do you want a blanket?

Potter To cover him up until the doctor arrives.

Linda (*rising in alarm*) Doctor?

Potter He fell off his ladder!

Linda (*without thinking*) Oh, the poor darling! (*She moves away a little in despair*)

Gerald Poor darling? Anyone would think that *you* were his girl-friend! (*He laughs*)

Linda No! Of course I'm not! Is he all right, Mr Potter?

Potter Well, I don't think anything's broken. Fortunately for him he landed on top of the kitchen refuse.

Linda }
Sandra } (*together*) What?!

Potter Yes! Big black bags of it! And I'm afraid they all split open under the impact! So he doesn't smell as sweetly as he should ...

Rodney comes in, unsteadily, UR. He is shaken and exhausted. His face and clothes (Gerald's clothes) are streaked with dirt, and various bits of stale salad adorn him

Potter goes to him, anxiously. Sandra goes to join Linda, with a quizzical smile

Mr Smith! You shouldn't be standing up! I left you lying down!

Rodney Go away! I'm all right! Oh, no, I'm not ...

He goes weak at the knees, but Potter supports him, perilously

Gerald (*going to assist*) We'd better get you up to your room. (*He reacts*) Ooh, you *do* stink! And look what you've done to my clothes!

Sandra (*quietly, to Linda*) Is *this* yours?

Linda Yes ...

Sandra I thought he'd gone?

Linda He came back ...

Sandra Well, he doesn't look very sexy *now*, does he? (*She giggles*)

Gerald and Potter pick Rodney up, one on either side

Gerald Right, son! What's the number of your room?

Linda He can't remember!

Gerald How do *you* know?

Sandra He's just fallen off a ladder!

Potter Yes! Probably got amnesia!

Gerald (*glaring at Potter*) Well, *you* haven't got amnesia!

Potter Yes, I have!

They put Rodney down again

Gerald Then go and look in the register!

Potter I can't!

Gerald Why not?

Potter Miss Figgis locked up and left.

Gerald Well, you're the manager! You must have a spare key!
Potter I've mislaid it! (*He escapes towards the seat*)

Gerald puts Rodney down on the sun lounger and glares at Potter

Gerald Well, we can't leave him *here*, can we?
Linda (*suddenly*) *I* know!

They all look at Linda

He can come and lie down in *my* room for the time being!
Gerald Good idea!

Linda runs to Rodney, eagerly

Potter (*appalled*) No!!
Gerald Why not? There's nowhere else until we find his *own* room. *I* can't even get back over the car park!
Potter No! I won't have immorality on the premises!
Gerald Don't be daft! There won't be anything immoral about it.
Linda (*disappointed*) Won't there?
Gerald No, of course not. He can go into your room—and you can move in with Sandra.

Linda and Sandra both look far from pleased

Sandra But if Linda's in my room with me—where are *you* going to be, Mr Corby? (*She smiles at him, mischievously*)

Gerald glares at her. Linda goes to her father, surprised

Linda Daddy! You aren't *really*——?
Gerald No, I'm not!
Sandra Yes, he is!
Linda Whatever will Mummy say when she finds out?
Gerald She's not *going* to find out! I mean—there's nothing to find out! It was all a mistake! Potter's sorting it out. Aren't you, Potter?
Potter I'm *trying* to ... (*He sits on the padded seat and thinks, deeply*)
Linda That's settled, then! (*To Rodney*) Come on!

Rodney looks up, still dazed from his fall

Rodney Where am I going?
Linda (*with a big smile*) You're coming to my bedroom.
Rodney Am I?
Linda (*as if just realizing*) Oh, I'm sorry! We haven't been introduced, have we? I'm Linda. And you're ... ?
Rodney (*dreamily*) Rodney ...
Linda Come on, then, Rodney!

Linda drags the weary, dazed Rodney off towards the bedrooms

Gerald glares at Sandra

Gerald What did you go and say that for? Now my daughter thinks I'm sharing a bedroom with *you*!

Sandra That's better than her thinking you're sharing with the plumber! (*She giggles*)
Gerald I'm not sharing with either of you!
Sandra Well, your toothbrush is still in my bathroom ...
Gerald (*alarmed*) Is it?
Sandra Yes—(*romantically*) right next to mine ...
Gerald It won't be much longer! (*He starts to go*)

Potter comes suddenly out of his reverie ...

Potter I've got it, Mr Corby!
Gerald (*hesitating*) What?
Potter For the time being you can move into your daughter's room with the other gentleman.
Sandra No, he can't!
Gerald Well done, Potter! I'll go and get my toothbrush. (*He starts to go*)
Sandra You don't have to be in such a hurry.
Potter Oh, yes, he does ... !

   Gerald exits

Sandra (*following Gerald*) Wait for me! I'll come and help you.
Potter No! He can manage on his own!
Sandra Well, he's not going to! Don't be such a spoilsport. (*Calling*) Mr Corby ... !

   Sandra runs out after Gerald

Potter (*miserably*) Oh, dear. The pillars of morality are starting to tremble again ...

   Potter hastens out after them towards the bedrooms

In the bedroom ...

   The door opens with the same flood of romantic music that we heard before, and Rodney and Linda come in. We see that the number "10" is on the outside of the door

Rodney is still exhausted after his escapade. He sinks on to the end of the bed and tries to gather himself. Linda closes the door and goes to draw the curtains. The room darkens a little. She turns on the bedside lamp. Then she kneels in front of him and gazes, romantically, into his bleak face. The music fades

Linda Oh, Rodney ...
Rodney H'm?
Linda Alone at last ...
Rodney (*the picture of dejection*) What?
Linda Now we've nothing to worry about ...
Rodney (*bleakly*) Haven't we?
Linda Daddy's got other things on his mind now.
Rodney Has he?

Linda So ... that's all right, isn't it?
Rodney Is it?
Linda Well, Rodney ... what did we come here for?

Rodney just manages to remember

Rodney Oh—that ...
Linda Yes!

Not unnaturally, Rodney finds it hard to be enthusiastic at this particular moment

Rodney Linda ...
Linda (*hopefully*) Yes?
Rodney I've just fallen off a ladder.
Linda I know. Poor darling ...
Rodney Well ... after you ... fall off a ladder, you do tend not to feel quite so ... romantic as you might.
Linda (*getting up, abruptly, and glaring at him*) You don't fancy me! Is that it?
Rodney No!
Linda You *don't*?!
Rodney I mean—no, it isn't that! Of course I fancy you.
Linda Well, this is the moment we've been waiting for—we're all alone and my father's out of the way—so why don't you get on with it?
Rodney I'm covered in cabbage ... !
Linda (*enraptured*) *I* don't mind ...
Rodney *I* do! Look—I'd rather ... freshen up a little first. If that's all the same to you.
Linda (*rather coolly*) All right. If you insist. I *suppose* I can wait ...
Rodney Oh. Right. Thanks. (*He goes with a weary tread to the bathroom where he turns, hopefully*) I say—is that Chinese food still here?
Linda (*livid*) How can you think of food at a time like this?
Rodney I'm hungry ... !

Far from pleased, Linda looks under the bed

Linda It's gone!
Rodney Gone where?
Linda *I* don't know! It would have been cold by now, anyway.
Rodney (*miserably*) I wouldn't have minded ...
Linda You mean you'd rather have cold Chinese food than hot *me*?
Rodney It's not that——!
Linda If food is all you fancy, I'll go and get you some grapes!

She storms out, furious, closing the door behind her, abruptly

Rodney sighs, and goes, aching, into the bathroom

The door to the corridor opens and Gerald comes in urgently followed by Sandra. We see that the number "14" is now on the outside of the door

Sandra Mr Corby! You don't have to move into Number Ten!
Gerald I'm not staying here! (*He goes towards the bathroom*)

Sandra locks the door. He looks alarmed

What are you doing?
Sandra We don't want anyone to interrupt us, do we?
Gerald There's nothing *to* interrupt! I only came back for my toothbrush.
Sandra Well, I see you've drawn the curtains already ...
Gerald What? (*He looks and the curtains are indeed drawn!*) Oh, my God ...!

He races across and draws back the curtains. The room lightens a little. Then he goes to switch off the lamp

It's a good thing my wife isn't still here ...
Sandra But she *is*!
Gerald What?!
Sandra (*sweetly logical*) And she's never going to believe that nothing happened—so let's *make* it happen!

She grabs him and pulls him on to the bed on top of her. Gerald struggles, manfully

The bathroom door opens and Marion walks in. She goes to peer at the struggling mass on the bed

Marion Are you looking for your toothbrush? (*She holds out a green toothbrush*)

Gerald stares, dismally, at the toothbrush, still in the grip of Sandra

Gerald That's not mine. Mine's yellow.
Marion No, darling. You always travel with your green one. You leave the yellow one at home. (*To Sandra, graciously*) Sandra I'm *so* sorry I interrupted——
Sandra So am I ... !

A loud knock at the door

Marion Good heavens! There's another one arriving! It must be the night shift coming on. (*She puts the toothbrush down on the armchair table*)

Gerald hastily extricates himself from Sandra's clutches

Potter (*off*) Mr Corby!
Marion Whatever does *he* want?

Gerald goes and opens the door

Potter is there, carrying Gerald's travel bag

Potter I hope you're ready to move, sir?
Gerald (*irritably*) All right, Potter—I'm coming!

Potter sees Marion, puts down the bag and goes to her in horror

Potter I thought you'd gone, madam.

Marion So did *he*! Gerry darling—why don't you tell us what you were doing in your secretary's bedroom?

Sandra He was giving me a little dictation.

Marion Dictation? You were rolling about on the bed together!

Potter turns to look at Gerald, appalled

Potter Oh, Mr Corby ... ! You'd only been in here for two minutes!

Gerald I wouldn't have been in here at all if it hadn't been for the plumber.

Marion What's the plumber got to do with it?

Potter He was so tired, poor man. Fifty miles he'd travelled. On his bicycle!

Marion What's a pedalling plumber got to do with my husband cavorting about on a bed with his secretary?

Potter After fifty miles he was too tired to see to the pipes.

Gerald So Miss Figgis popped the plumber into *my* room.

Marion And you popped into Sandra's room!

Gerald I didn't know it was Sandra's room!

Sandra (*smiling*) *I* did ... !

Marion And where is the plumber now?

Potter Seeing to the boiler.

Gerald (*pleased*) Oh, good!

Marion I don't believe a word of it.

Potter It's true. I saw him going down there with his spanner. (*He picks up Gerald's travel bag*) Shall we go, then, sir?

Gerald What?

Potter To room Number *Ten*! (*He goes to the door*)

Gerald Ah—yes—right! Just coming, Potter.

Marion But Number Ten is Linda's room.

Potter (*sagely*) Oh, it's all change here now, madam.

Potter smiles, faintly, and goes

Gerald is about to follow

Marion (*severely*) You don't think I'm such a fool as to *believe* all this, do you?

Gerald Yes.

Marion Well, I'm not! (*She marches to the door*)

Gerald But it's the truth!

Marion turns at the door

Marion Poor Gerry ... It must have been bad enough finding that your secretary was *staying* here without having to share a room with her, as well! (*She opens the door*)

Gerald Where are you going?

Marion I told you—to visit an old friend.

Gerald It's a bit late now, isn't it? What time was she expecting you?

Marion smiles, enigmatically

Marion *She*? Whatever gave you the idea it was a woman?

Gerald What?

Marion goes, closing the door behind her

Gerald looks astonished. Sandra laughs and goes to him, happily

Sandra There! You see? You needn't have worried, Mr Corby.
Gerald What do you mean?
Sandra Well, if *she*'s going to see another feller, *we* can carry on from where we left off! (*She tries to embrace him*)
Gerald (*evading her*) No, we can't! (*He goes to the door, quickly*) I'm getting out of here!
Sandra Won't you stay and try one of my grapes?
Gerald No fear!

He stumbles out, and closes the door with a bang

Fed up, Sandra starts to go towards the bathroom, then notices the toothbrush on the armchair table. She picks it up and goes into the bathroom, smiling delightedly

There is a knock at the corridor door. Rodney now comes out of the bathroom. He has cleaned himself up and is back in the short dressing-gown. He seems to have regained his enthusiasm for what he came here for

Rodney Coming, darling! (*Smiling happily, he opens the door*) I'm feeling much more like it now!

Marion is there. His smile fades. We see that the number "10" is now on the outside of the door. Marion smiles

Marion Oh, I *am* glad! (*She comes into the room*) But what are you doing in Number Ten? This is my daughter's bedroom.

Rodney shuts the door and follows her, nervously

Rodney She lent it to me! Said I could have a bath and freshen up.
Marion And that's why you're feeling more like it?
Rodney Well . . .
Marion (*approvingly*) Oh, yes—that's much better. . . .
Rodney Sorry?
Marion Now you've taken off my husband's trousers.
Rodney Ah—yes. I fell off the ladder, you see.
Marion Oh . . . !
Rodney (*anxious to be rid of her*) Well, I—I'll tell Linda that you called——
Marion There's no hurry. I can wait. (*She sits in the armchair*)
Rodney Can you? Oh, dear . . . (*He glances, anxiously, towards the door*)
Marion Who did you think I was?
Rodney Sorry?
Marion Just now when I knocked at the door.
Rodney Oh, I . . . I thought perhaps my girl-friend had found me!

Marion smiles, suspiciously

Marion *I* don't think you've *got* a girl-friend . . .
Rodney W-what?
Marion *I* think you're here all on your own . . .
Rodney No! Really! I—er. . . .

Marion rises and moves towards him, seductively. Rodney backs away, nervously

Marion And that's why you keep climbing up ladders and getting into people's bedrooms . . .
Rodney No! No, of course not!
Marion Oh, don't apologize. There's nothing wrong with it . . .
Rodney Isn't there?
Marion *I* think it's rather exciting . . .
Rodney D-do you?
Marion *I* wouldn't complain if you came in through *my* bedroom window . . .
Rodney W-wouldn't you?
Marion (*smiling, disturbingly*) What's the matter? You're not frightened of older women, are you?
Rodney No—no, I . . .
Marion I'm so glad!

She grabs him, enthusiastically, and pulls him down on to the bed on top of her. He struggles, manfully

The door opens, and Gerald walks in, carrying a bunch of grapes

Gerald Would you like a bunch of grapes?

Then he sees them on the bed

Marion No, thank you, Gerry. I think we've got everything we want.

Rodney disentangles himself from Marion and escapes away to the armchair, deeply embarrassed. Marion remains sitting serenely on the bed

Gerald (*frostily*) I thought you were going off to meet your "friend"!
Marion I'm on my way.
Gerald I can see that! (*He glares at Rodney*)
Marion I just popped in to say goodbye to Linda.
Gerald And said hallo to *him* instead?
Rodney It . . . it wasn't as bad as you think.
Gerald (*going to Rodney*) Oh, good! Perhaps you'll give her a reference? What the hell do you think you were doing?
Marion Wasn't that obvious?
Gerald (*to Rodney*) You were lent this room to recover after your fall, not to attack defenceless unaccompanied married females!
Marion Oh, dear. Is that what I am?
Gerald (*to Marion*) Didn't you remember that you'd got a husband here?
Marion You've got a *wife* here, but it didn't stop *you* . . .

The door opens and Potter comes in with a bunch of grapes and Gerald's travel bag

Potter I thought the young man would feel better for some grapes. (*He sees Marion*) Mrs Corby! You're still here!
Marion I'm just leaving!

Potter puts down the travel bag and goes to Rodney, concerned

Potter Oh, sir—you're supposed to be lying down.
Gerald He *was*—on the bed with my wife!
Potter What?! (*To Rodney, appalled*) You were lying on a bed with a defenceless unaccompanied married female?
Marion Don't *you* start!
Potter Poor Mrs Corby. Oh, I shall have to sit down. (*He sits down next to Marion*) What an ordeal . . . (*He eats a grape*)
Marion You don't have to worry. (*Disappointed*) My husband came in before anything happened.
Potter But the shock! Would *you* like a grape, Mrs Corby? I'm sure you're ready for one.
Marion Oh, thank you, Mr Potter. You're quite a gentleman, after all.

Potter and Marion eat grapes

Gerald (*seething*) Look, Potter! The sooner you find this young man's own room the better, then he can concentrate on his *own* girl-friend and keep his hands off other people's women!
Marion (*to Potter*) Now I'm "other people's women" . . . !

The door opens and Linda comes in, carrying a bunch of grapes

Linda Here you are! Perhaps *these* will make you feel a bit sexier! (*She holds out the grapes*)

She sees them all. They see her. Reactions

I . . . I brought him some grapes . . .
Potter It'll soon be like a vineyard in here.
Linda Mummy, you're still here!
Gerald Yes. You mustn't keep your "friend" waiting!
Marion (*to Potter*) It's so bad for the morale when people keep asking you to leave.
Potter You come with me, Mrs Corby. (*They start to go*) Perhaps you'd like a nice cup of tea before you go? It'll settle your nerves. They must be in ribbons. I know mine are.

Potter and Marion go, he taking the grapes with him

Linda (*hopefully*) Aren't *you* going, too, Daddy?
Gerald Going? I'm moving in with *him*?
Linda What?!
Gerald Got no choice, have I? Thanks to that wretched plumber I've got to share a room with a sex maniac!

Linda He's not that!

Gerald Yes, he is! Just now he was rolling about on the bed with your mother!

Linda What?! (*Glaring at Rodney*) *Were* you?

Rodney Well ... yes ...

Linda (*appalled*) *Yes*?!

Rodney In a way.

Linda In a way?!

Rodney It wasn't my idea!

Linda But you don't deny it?

Rodney No, but it wasn't——!

Linda Right! (*She starts to go*)

Rodney Where are you going?

Linda I'm not staying here with a sex-mad window cleaner.

Linda goes, quickly, slamming the door behind her

Gerald I can't think why *she*'s so upset. You were lucky your girl-friend didn't find out what you were up to.

Rodney I wasn't up to anything!

Gerald Now look son—you take my advice——

Rodney I took your advice before and see where it landed me!

Rodney races out after Linda, slamming the door behind him

Gerald shrugs, picks up his travel bag and goes out into the bathroom

In the pool area ...

Potter and Marion wander in from DL, *eating grapes*

Potter We'll get you a nice strong cup of tea, Mrs Corby. It must have been such a shock for you.

Marion (*suffering suitably*) Oh, it *was*, Mr Potter ...

Potter And for *me*. ...

Marion Why you?

Potter I never thought I'd live to see the day when the moral supports of this establishment were on the brink of collapse ...

Linda comes storming in, still seething with anger. She strides across, opens the door to the steam bath (from which a puff of steam erupts), goes inside and slams the door shut

Potter considers this

I had no idea she was down for a steam bath at this time ...

Rodney races in from the bedrooms

Marion clings on to the astonished Potter in mock fear

Marion Ooh! He's coming after me again!

Rodney stops, seeing Marion, turns and runs out the way he came in

Marion is a little aggrieved

Oh. He must have changed his mind.

Potter (*thoughtfully*) I only hope he doesn't go into the lounge dressed like that ...

He extricates himself from Marion as ...

Linda bursts out of the steam bath

Linda There's a man in there with his clothes on!

She runs out through the archway to the bedrooms

Potter It'll be the plumber. He's here to fix the boiler.

As they continue on their way, Potter looks down at his grapes, despondently

Oh, Mrs Corby, you've squashed my grapes ...

They disappear through the archway UR

In the bedroom ...

Rodney comes in, urgently. We see the number "14" on the door

Rodney Linda! Are you in here?

Sandra comes out of the bathroom, sees him and smiles, hopefully

Sandra Oo! Is it my birthday?

Rodney Sorry! I didn't mean to——

Sandra Don't worry. His wife's frightened him off, so I'm all alone ...

Rodney No, no! I'm looking for Linda! I thought she might be with you.

Sandra No—she's not. Won't *I* do? (*She runs to him and puts her arms around him, eagerly*)

Rodney (*resisting*) Sandra! What are you playing at?

Sandra Oh, come on! Don't be such a spoilsport ... (*She cuddles close to him*)

Rodney No!

Sandra You don't have to worry. If someone comes in we'll say we're dancing. (*She clings to him like a limpet*)

And at that moment Linda walks in and sees them

Linda Rodney!!

Rodney leaps away from Sandra

You're at it again! Are you sex mad?

Sandra (*smiling, happily*) Oh, yes ... !

Linda Not you! *Him*!

Rodney Of course I'm not!

Linda Well, every time I come into a bedroom you're with a different woman! What were you doing?

Rodney Dancing!

Linda You expect me to believe that?

Sandra (*unhappily*) It's true. I tried to get him to do it, but he wouldn't . . .
Linda Do *what*?!
Rodney Practise the rhumba!

Sandra suddenly thinks of something, and cheers up immediately

Sandra Ooh—wait a minute—if you're both in here, Mr Corby must be all alone in Number Ten! (*She giggles and scuttles out, optimistically*)

Linda and Rodney are alone again

Linda Wouldn't you?
Rodney What?
Linda Practise the rhumba with Sandra.
Rodney Of course I wouldn't! I came here to practise with *you*! And all I've done so far is climb up and down ladders, in and out of bedroom windows, and fall up to my neck in kitchen waste!

She smiles at him, warmly

Linda Well, don't let's waste any more time, then . . . (*She starts to embrace him, pulling him towards the bed*)
Rodney But this is Number Fourteen. We're supposed to be in Number Ten.
Linda What difference does it make? They both look exactly the same . . .

They embrace and fall back on to the bed

The door opens and Gerald walks in, talking as he arrives and heading for the bathroom

Gerald I think I left my toothbrush in here—— (*He stops, reacts and turns to look at them*) Linda! What are you doing?
Linda (*patiently*) We're two adults consenting, and we *thought* we were in private.
Gerald (*to Rodney*) Are you some kind of sex maniac? First you're on the bed with my wife and now with my daughter!
Rodney I'm trying to get into the Guinness Book of Records.

In the pool area . . .

Potter and Marion come in from the archway UR. *He is carrying a tray of tea things*

Potter Here we are, Mrs Corby. A small pot of tea. You sit down and make yourself comfortable.

Marion sits on the padded seat. Potter puts the tray on the garden table and carries it down to her. He puts it down and sits beside her

You'll feel much better for a nice cup of tea. I know *I* will. (*He stirs the tea in the tiny pot, briskly, and starts to pour two cups*)
Gerald (*to Rodney*) You aren't even ashamed!
Rodney Why should I be?
Potter Sugar, Mrs Corby?
Gerald But you told me you'd already *got* a girlfriend here!

Marion No, thank you, Mr Potter.
Linda He has! It's *me*!
Potter Just one for me, then.

He empties the contents of the tiny sugar bowl into his cup and stirs it, vigorously

Gerald *You*?
Linda Yes.
Gerald You mean you *didn't* come here on your own?
Linda No.
Gerald You came with—with *him*?
Linda Yes.

Sandra comes in and sees Gerald. She smiles, delightedly

Sandra Oo, you're back in *my* room, Mr Corby! I looked for you in Number Ten.
Gerald I left my toothbrush behind!
Sandra Yes—I know ... !
Gerald (*to Linda*) You're not ... (*indicating Rodney*) ... sharing the same room?
Linda We're *trying* to!

Gerald looks about to erupt

Gerald But he's a *window-cleaner*!!
Marion Very nice tea, Mr Potter.
Potter I'm glad you liked it, Mrs Corby. I always use one spoonful for each person—(*he lifts up the tiny teapot*)—and just a *half* for the pot!

They laugh, happily

Gerald You came here with a—with a window-cleaner? You can't be serious!
Rodney But we are, Mr Corby! *Very* serious ...
Linda (*to Rodney, delighted*) Are we?
Rodney *Very* serious!
Gerald (*decisively*) Oh, no! No! I won't have that!
Sandra Oh yes, you will.

Gerald turns to look at Sandra, surprised by her intervention

Gerald What's it got to do with *you*?
Sandra (*innocently*) Well, why shouldn't they come here together? You and I did!
Gerald (*red-faced*) What are you talking about? You know very well we didn't come here together!
Sandra Oh, yes. *I* know that, and *you* know that. But your *wife* doesn't know that, does she?
Gerald (*aghast*) You wouldn't tell my wife something that wasn't true?
Sandra I might ...
Gerald That's blackmail!

Sandra Oh, good! I've never done that ...

She grins at him and runs out of the room, quickly

Gerald panics

Gerald Here! Where are you going? Oh, my God ... !

He runs out after Sandra

Linda looks at Rodney, happily

Linda You never said you were ... serious.
Rodney I'm a window-cleaner. I'm always serious.

They kiss and follow the others, closing the door behind them

Potter and Marion look up from their tea as—

Sandra races in with Gerald in hot pursuit

Marion (*wearily*) Oh, Gerry, you're not chasing her *again*, are you?
Gerald No, I'm not! (*He pretends to be skipping*)
Potter Well I hope you're not expecting tea. I've only made a pot for two ...
Sandra Mrs Corby—there's something I think I ought to tell you ...
Gerald (*loudly*) No, there isn't!!
Marion (*astonished*) Gerry! Whatever's the matter?

Rodney and Linda come in

Potter (*seeing them*) Oh, dear. Two more! I should have made a larger pot ...
Sandra Go on, then, Mr Corby—*you* tell her!
Gerald (*giving in*) Oh, all right ...

They all watch, intrigued, as Gerald gathers himself and tries to appear cheerful as he prepares to make a great pronouncement

I've got some ... *wonderful* news for you, Marion.
Marion (*to Potter*) It *must* be serious. He's calling me Marion.
Gerald (*continuing, inexorably*) My little girl ...
Marion Which one is that?
Gerald Linda!
Marion Oh, *that* little girl ...

Linda and Sandra giggle

Gerald My little girl ... didn't come here ... *alone*. She came here ... (*desperately cheerful*) ... with a *window-cleaner*!
Marion (*alarmed*) What?
Linda It's true, Mummy. (*She links arms with Rodney, happily*)

Marion jumps to her feet in surprise, knocking over her cup. Potter hastily mops up

Potter Oh, Mrs Corby ... ! All over my trousers!

Marion Not . . . *this* window-cleaner?
Linda Yes! *My* window-cleaner . . . (*She gazes at Rodney, adoringly*)
Marion Oh, my God . . . !
Gerald (*maintaining his excessive bonhomie*) Isn't that wonderful news? My
    little girl's sharing a room—with *Rodney*!
Marion (*astonished*) And you don't mind?

Gerald forces a delighted smile

Gerald Of course I don't mind!
Potter Well, you *should* mind . . . !
Marion (*to Linda*) You . . . you came here together, then?
Linda } (*together*) Yes!
Rodney
Sandra Which is more than *we* did—eh, Mr Corby?

*Gerald looks at her, gratefully, and points her out to Marion, jumping about
with nervous relief*

Gerald Ah! Yes! There! There—you see? (*He kisses Marion on the forehead*)
    Did you hear that? Did you hear what she said? (*He kisses Potter on the
    forehead*) We didn't come here together! What did I tell you? (*He kisses
    Sandra on the forehead, then realizes who he is kissing and hastily backs
    away*)
Marion (*going to him*) Gerry, there's no need to get so excited.
Gerald Isn't there?
Marion I *know* you didn't come here together. (*She smiles, warmly*)
Gerald Oh, good!
Marion (*suddenly severe*) But you still ended up in the same bedroom.

They all enjoy Gerald's discomfort

Gerald Here—wait a minute! Why should *I* feel guilty? What about you?
    Who is this *man* you're going to visit?
Potter (*distressed*) Oh, no, Mrs Corby! Not *you*, as well . . . ! (*He concen-
    trates, bleakly, on his tea*)
Linda Don't you tell him, Mummy.
Marion (*mock serious*) I wouldn't dream of it . . .
Gerald Who *is* he?!

Marion smiles, enigmatically

Marion Wouldn't you like to know . . . ! (*Then, warmly*) Oh, Gerry . . . ! (*She
    embraces him*)
Linda Oh, Rodney . . . ! (*She embraces him*)

Sandra turns to Potter, smiling optimistically

Sandra Oh, Potter . . . !

Potter looks up from his tea in alarm

Potter Oh, no . . . !

As he tries unsuccessfully to escape from Sandra's embracing arms, there is a sudden loud explosion from within the steam baths. They all react as—

The door bursts open and the Plumber staggers out. His clothes are torn and dirty, his face streaked with black. Without noticing anyone, he staggers across and disappears through the archway DL

They all watch him in astonishment, and then start to laugh as the music swells and——

—the CURTAIN *falls*

FURNITURE AND PROPERTY LIST

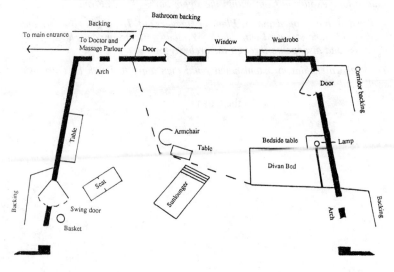

ACT I

On stage:

Poolside area:
Sun lounger
Colourful padded seat. *On it:* **Sandra**'s towel
Low garden table
White wicker laundry basket
Signs "To the Doctor" and "To Massage Parlour"
Tiled floor

Bedroom:
Recessed wardrobe cupboard. *In it:* some of **Sandra**'s clothes (as dressing),
    perfume atomizer
Divan bed
Duvet and cover
Pillows and pillow cases
Small bedside table. *On it:* telephone, lamp
Small armchair
Small table
Door numbers 10 and 14 (interchangeable)
Window curtains (open)
Carpet

Off stage: 3 towels **(Gerald)**
Weekend bag **(Rodney)**. *In it:* various items of clothing, washbag, transis-
    tor radio
Beach towel **(Linda,** *bathroom)*
Bikini **(Linda,** *bathroom)*
Clipboard **(Potter)**

Mug of Bovril **(Sandra)**
Short feminine dressing-gown (**Rodney**, *bathroom*)
Glass of orange juice **(Gerald)**
Man's pyjama trousers (**Rodney**, *bathroom*)
Towelling robe (**Potter**, for **Sandra**)
Health farm register (dust inside) **(Potter)**
Man's pyjama jacket (**Gerald**, *bathroom*)

Personal: **Rodney**: Dark sun-glasses, wristwatch
Potter: pen
Marion: Handbag

ACT II

Off stage: Tea-cup ($\frac{1}{2}$ full), saucer, teaspoon **(Marion)**
Travel bag **(Gerald)**
Jacket, trousers, shirt **(Gerald)**
Bottle of red wine **(Sandra)**
Man's dressing-gown (**Gerald**, *bathroom*)
2 plastic glasses (**Sandra**, *bathroom*)
Towel **(Linda)**
Plastic shopping bag. *In it:* silver foil containers (full) **(Rodney)**
Sundress (**Linda**, *bathroom*)
2 pairs chopsticks **(Rodney)**
Bottle opener **(Rodney)**
Towel **(Sandra)**
Bits of stale salad **(Rodney)**
Green toothbrush (**Marion**, *bathroom*)
Bunch of grapes **(Gerald)**
Bunch of grapes **(Potter)**
Bunch of grapes **(Linda)**
Tea tray. *On it:* small teapot, small sugar bowl (with sugar), 2 tea cups and
saucers, milk jug, napkin **(Potter)**

Personal: **Gerald**: £5 note
Potter: Handkerchief

LIGHTING PLOT

Property fittings required: a bedside lamp

Interior. A composite set of swimming-pool area and a bedroom. The same scene throughout

ACT I   Summer evening

To open: Black-out

Cue 1	As CURTAIN rises *Bring up lights in pool area*	(Page 1)
Cue 2	**Gerald:** "Oh, my God . . . !" *Bring up lights in bedroom*	(Page 6)
Cue 3	As **Linda** goes to look out into the corridor *Lights out in bedroom*	(Page 27)
Cue 4	As **Potter** goes out DL *Bring up lights in bedroom*	(Page 27)
Cue 5	**Potter** falls on to the sun lounger *Black-out*	(Page 39)

ACT II   The same

To open: Black-out

Cue 6	As CURTAIN rises *Bring up lights in all areas*	(Page 40)
Cue 7	**Sandra** draws the curtains *Lower bedroom lighting slightly*	(Page 47)
Cue 8	**Sandra** switches on bedside lamp *Switch on lamp lighting*	(Page 47)
Cue 9	**Gerald** draws back the curtains *Bedroom lighting back to full*	(Page 49)
Cue 10	**Gerald** turns off bedside lamp *Switch off lamp lighting*	(Page 49)
Cue 11	**Linda:** "What?!" *Black-out bedroom lights*	(Page 59)
Cue 12	As **Gerald** and **Potter** go *Lights up in bedroom*	(Page 60)
Cue 13	**Linda** draws the curtains *Lower bedroom lighting slightly*	(Page 70)

EFFECTS PLOT

ACT I

Cue 1   As CURTAIN rises   (Page 1)
Peaceful, relaxing music

Cue 2   **Gerald** staggers out   (Page 1)
Puff of steam

Cue 3   **Gerald** "Aren't you going to take your trousers off?"   (Page 2)
Fade out music

Cue 4   **Gerald** goes into the steam bath   (Page 3)
Puff of steam

Cue 5   **Gerald** disappears into his towelling   (Page 4)
Fade in romantic music (if possible "Love is a Many-Splendoured   Thing")

Cue 6   **Gerald**: "Aaaah!"   (Page 5)
Cut music

Cue 7   **Gerald** disapears into his towelling again   (Page 14
Fade in romantic music as before

Cue 8   **Gerald**: "Aaaah"   (Page 14)
Cut music

ACT II

Cue 9   As CURTAIN rises   (Page 40)
Fade out theme music

Cue 10   As **Potter** goes towards the bedrooms   (Page 47)
Fade in romantic music as before

Cue 11   **Gerald** sees **Sandra** lying on the bed   (Page 47)
Cut music

Cue 12   **Gerald** kisses **Marion** also   (Page 52)
Lavatory flushes in the bathroom

Cue 13   **Linda** goes into the bathroom   (Page 56)
Fade in romantic music as before

Cue 14   **Linda** returns   (Page 56)
Fade out music

Cue 15   As **Potter** goes towards the bedrooms   (Page 70)
Fade in romantic music as before

MADE AND PRINTED IN GREAT BRITAIN BY
LATIMER TREND & COMPANY LTD PLYMOUTH

MADE IN ENGLAND